HOW TO BUY
A HOUSE

If you want to know how . . .

Getting the Builders In
How to manage homebuilding and renovation projects

Buying a Property in France
An insider guide to realising your dream

How to Make Money from Property
The expert guide to property investment

How to be a Property Millionaire

Send for a free copy of the latest catalogue to:

How To Books
3 Newtec Place, Magdalan Road,
Oxford OX4 1RE
email:info@howtobooks.co.uk
http://www.howtobooks.co.uk

HOW TO BUY
A HOUSE

SAVE MONEY AND REDUCE STRESS
BUYING YOUR IDEAL HOME

REVISED AND UPDATED·
2ND
·SECOND EDITION·

A D A M   W A L K E R

howtobooks

Published by How To Books Ltd,
3 Newtec Place, Magdalen Road,
Oxford OX4 1RE. United Kingdom.
Tel: (01865) 793806. Fax: (01865) 248780.
email: info@howtobooks.co.uk
www.howtobooks.co.uk

First edition 1999
Reprinted 2000
Reprinted with amendments 2001
Reprinted 2002
Reprinted 2003
Second edition 2006

British Library Cataloguing in Publication Data
A catalogue record for this book is available from the British
Library

Cover design by Baseline Arts Ltd, Oxford
Produced for How To Books by Deer Park Productions
Typeset by Anneset, Weston-super-Mare, Somerset
Printed and bound by Cromwell Press, Trowbridge, Wiltshire

NOTE: The material contained in this book is set out in good
faith for general guidance and no liability can be accepted for
loss or expense incurred as a result of relying in particular
circumstances on statements made in the book. The laws and
regulations are complex and liable to change, and readers
should check the current position with the relevant authorities
before making personal arrangements.

Contents

List of Illustrations

Acknowledgements

This book would have not been possible without the help of a great many people. In particular I would like to thank the Woolwich Building Society for allowing me to use their average cost of moving survey and my secretary Lyn Harding for her patience, good humour and attention to detail during each draft of this book.

In this book please read he to mean he or she.

Preface

This book is a thoroughly practical guide to buying a house. If you are buying for the first time the book will guide you step by step through the whole process and help to ensure that you buy the right property in the right area at the right price. If you have a bought a property before this book will explain how the new home buying process is likely to work and help to ensure you gain the maximum negotiating advantage at each stage of your purchase.

FORTHCOMING LEGISTLATION

The government intends to make radical changes to the house buying process. From 2007 it will become an offence to market a property without first preparing a Home information pack. The Home information pack will include:

◆ copy **title deeds**
◆ replies to standard **enquiries**
◆ replies to standard **searches**
◆ a **survey** report.

The cost of providing this information for a typical property will be £500 to £700. This will have to be paid by the seller *before* their property can be put onto the market. The consequences of this legislation will be very far reaching.

◆ In future, buyers may be able to exchange contracts on the spot. At the moment it takes around eight weeks.

- In future, costs will be borne by the seller. At the moment they are borne by the purchaser.
- In future, all legal work will be completed before the house is put onto the market. At the moment it is not done until after a buyer has been found.

I have made numerous references to the new legislation throughout this book and I have tried to assess the likely consequences of the new Home information pack to both buyers and sellers.

Adam Walker

①
Buying Versus Renting

This is the most important question in the whole of this book:

Are you absolutely certain that you want to buy a property at this time?

Many people who became home owners during the 1980s did so because there was no viable alternative. The result of anti-landlord legislation passed in 1977 was that there were few privately owned properties available to rent during the 1980s. This left most people with a choice between joining a long waiting list to rent a council or housing association owned property, or buying their own home. The consequence was that by 1988 home ownership levels in the United Kingdom had risen to almost 70 per cent, one of the highest rates in the developed world.

Today the situation is completely different. The Housing Act, which was passed in 1988, made letting a property a much more attractive proposition for landlords and today there is a plentiful supply of good quality privately owned property available to rent in most areas. Before you commit yourself to buying a property, consider the alternative of renting.

RENTING A PROPERTY: KEY ADVANTAGES
Staying flexible
The most important advantage of rented property is its flexibility. Most tenancies are of six or 12 months duration. At the end of this period you can walk away without any further cost or obligation. If your future plans are uncertain, you may find that renting a property is a much better bet.

Moving fast
It is usually possible to move into a rented property within a few days of seeing it. Buying a property usually takes three to four months. If you are in a hurry to move, a rented property might be a useful stopgap.

Convenience
Repairs and maintenance are usually the responsibility of the landlord. This could be important if you work very long hours or don't have the inclination to undertake or supervise repairs. It also makes it easier to plan your budget accurately.

CASE STUDY
David and Karen rush into buying a house
David M was asked to move from Yorkshire to west London by his employer. He and his wife Karen spent a whole week looking for a property to buy. Prices in west London were far higher than in Yorkshire and it quickly became clear that they would have to make some compromises. After looking at more than 40 houses in six days they bought a house in a village about ten miles west of his new office at Heathrow. Within days of moving in they regretted their decision. The village, which had

seemed quite pleasant during the day, was full of rowdy teenagers during the evenings. The journey to work took much longer than David had expected – an hour and five minutes to do ten miles. Worst of all the head-master of their daughter's new primary school was unable to recommend any good secondary school in the area.

After a thoroughly unhappy first year they sold up and moved to a smaller house in a much nicer village five miles away.

Commenting on his experience, David says 'We bought the first house in far too much of a hurry. With hindsight I wish that we had rented somewhere for the first six months and got to know the area properly. The extra move has cost us thousands of pounds and caused a great deal of unnecessary stress and frustration.'

OWNING A PROPERTY: KEY ADVANTAGES
Capital growth
If you rent a property for 25 years, you will end up with nothing. If you buy the property on a 25-year mortgage, at the end of the **mortgage** term you will own it outright. The opportunity to achieve a capital gain in this way is, for many home owners, the single most important factor behind their decision to buy their own property.

Assessing cost
In the long term buying a property will probably cost less

than renting one. Most commercial landlords will be aiming to achieve a gross yield of around 8 per cent from their investment. This means that the owner of a property worth £100,000 will be hoping to achieve an annual rental of £100,000 x 8 per cent ie £8,000 per annum. Out of this the landlord will have to pay for repairs and maintenance and also, in most cases, a fee to the managing agents.

If you were to borrow money at, say, 6 per cent to buy a similar property your mortgage would be £100,000 x 6 per cent ie £6,000 per annum. (Due to the way that mortgage interest payments are calculated the true annual percentage rate of the loan may be higher than 6 per cent and the payments increased accordingly.) This gives a gross saving of £2,000 per annum out of which the cost of repairs and maintenance will have to be met.

Taking everything into account, it is usually cheaper to own a property than to rent one.

However, this is not always the case as average yields do vary significantly from property to property and from area to area. Landlords of cheaper properties generally expect to achieve higher yields than landlords of larger and/or more expensive properties.)

Another factor to take into account is the costs associated with buying and reselling a property. If you expect to stay in the property for less than two years it would probably be cheaper to rent than to buy.

CONSIDERING-NON FINANCIAL FACTORS

In addition to the financial arguments there are some important emotional factors to consider.

Being disrupted by repeated moves

Many rented properties are only available for a fixed term. If you choose to rent a property, you are far more likely to have to face the stress and disruption of further moves.

Decorating

You will not usually be allowed to change the decor of a rented property. Many people find that they cannot feel truly at home until they have decorated to their own taste.

Caring for furnishings

Most furnished properties come with carpets and curtains and many are fully or partly furnished. The need to be constantly careful to protect someone else's furnishings prevents many people from feeling fully at home in a rented property.

CASE STUDY
Philip continues renting for too long

Philip B moved from Manchester to east London with his job. The job move came up at short notice and Philip rented a two-bedroomed flat in the Docklands area because he did not have time to look for somewhere to buy.

Philip liked the flat so much that he extended the initial 12-month tenancy three times. After four years Philip's landlord gave him notice that he had decided to sell it. This prompted Philip to start looking for property to buy. He was horrified to find that prices had risen dramatically in the intervening four years.

Commenting on his experience, Philip says 'With hindsight I should have bought my own property years ago – as soon as it became apparent that I was going to stay in the London area. As a result of my dithering I have ended up paying much more than I needed to for my new home.'

FINDING A PROPERTY TO RENT
Using lettings/property management agents

In most areas there are one or more estate agents who specialise in rented property. Their service is free to prospective tenants so it is well worth registering your requirements with all the firms in the local area.

The agents will usually start by asking you some questions to ensure that you are a suitable prospective tenant. If you give the right answers, you will probably be told about suitable properties over the telephone and encouraged to view immediately. Property management is a very fast moving business and properties often come and go within a few hours. Because of this many agents do not prepare written particulars of the properties that are available for rent. Your decision to view will therefore usually have to be made on the basis of a phone call.

Agreeing a rent

Rents for apparently identical properties can vary enormously so it is worth shopping around by registering with more than one agent. Rents are often negotiable, so when you find somewhere that you like try an offer – you can always increase it if the landlord says no.

Providing references

Landlords fear two things:

◆ that you will not pay the rent
◆ that you will damage their property.

To protect themselves, most landlords will ask for financial, employment and personal references.

Signing tenancy agreements

Most tenancy agreements are now Assured Shorthold Tenancies. You commit to pay the agreed rent for the agreed period and the landlord guarantees you the right to occupy the property for the whole of the agreed term – usually six or 12 months.

Providing a deposit

Most landlords will require a deposit of at least one month's rent. The cost of any damage to the property will be deducted from this at the end of the term.

The failure to return deposits is a very common cause of disputes between landlords and tenants. The best way to safeguard your deposit is to arrange the tenancy through a reputable agent who can act as mediator in any future dispute. Most reputable lettings agents are members of the Association of Residential Letting Agents (ARLA). ARLA has strict rules over the handling of deposits by its members.

Checking in

Another precaution that you should take to safeguard your deposit is to make a careful inspection of the condition of the property at the start of the tenancy. Any damage should be pointed out to the landlord or the managing agent, recorded in writing and, if possible, photographed.

SUMMARY

Financially it is usually better to buy a property than to rent one. However, you should consider renting a property if you:

◆ are planning to move again in less than two years
◆ are moving to an unfamiliar area
◆ need to move very quickly
◆ do not have the time or inclination to deal with day-to-day maintenance and repairs
◆ are unsure of your future plans.

(2)

Understanding
the Process

The process for buying a property in England and Wales is horribly inefficient. The average time between an offer being accepted and completion is 12 weeks. This is twice as long as it takes in most other countries. Worse still, one third of all the sales that are agreed fail to reach completion. When a sale does fall through, buyers can be left with a bill for abortive costs of several thousand pounds.

The government has said that it intends to change the home buying process. From 2007 it will become an offence to market a property without first preparing a home information pack. The consequences of this will be very far reaching and are discussed in detail later in this book. However, until 2007 the house buying process will continue to work in much the same way as it has done for the last 300 years.

In view of this I will start this chapter explaining the current home buying process.

By gaining a better understanding of the process you will be able to avoid many of the most common pitfalls.

1. Select short list of areas

2. Look through local papers in order to assess property prices in the chosen area

3. Choose a mortgage broker and arrange a mortgage in principle

4. Choose a solicitor

5. If selling, instruct solicitor to obtain title deeds and prepare draft contract of sale of current property

6. If selling, put current property on market and wait for a sale to be agreed in principle

7. Contact all estate agents in the area and view a selection of properties

8. Make/agree offer to buy chosen property

9. Instruct solicitor to proceed with work on purchase

10. Instruct mortgage lender to proceed

Fig. 1. Recommended home buying process (current system)

UNDERSTANDING THE ROLE OF THE ESTATE AGENT

A survey found that estate agents are less popular than used-car salesmen, double glazing salesmen and even politicians. People love to hate their estate agent, but much of this antipathy arises because of a widespread misunderstanding of the estate agent's role.

An estate agent has a commercial, ethical and legal duty to work on behalf of his client, ie the vendor. This means getting the best price for the property, negotiating terms that are favourable to the vendor and acting in accordance with the vendor's instructions at all times.

As the purchaser, you should expect estate agents to be helpful and friendly towards you in order to encourage you to view the properties that they have available. But, however nice the estate agent is, you must never forget that their job is to act in the interests of the other side.

Knowing what to expect of an agent

The estate agent's main functions during the sale are to:

◆ Advise the vendor on the optimum asking price for the property.
◆ Prepare sales particulars and check their accuracy.
◆ Send particulars to all potential buyers on the mailing list.
◆ Follow up the particulars with a phone call in order to achieve the maximum number of viewings.
◆ Encourage interested potential purchasers to make an offer.

◆ Negotiate on the vendor's behalf to achieve the highest possible price.

◆ Qualify the buyer to make sure that they are in a position to proceed immediately with their purchase.

◆ (Sometimes) arrange mortgage finance on behalf of the buyer.

◆ Liaise with the purchaser, mortgage lender and both solicitors on a regular basis to ensure that the sale is proceeding smoothly.

UNDERSTANDING THE ROLE OF THE MORTGAGE LENDER

Most building societies were set up during Victorian times. Originally they were mutual organisations owned by their members and their objectives were largely altruistic. They paid a fair rate of interest to attract savers and used this money to help ordinary working people to buy their own homes. A hundred years ago very few people had any savings and building societies were the only possible source of mortgage funding for most would-be home buyers.

Today the situation is entirely different. Banks, insurance companies and specialised mortgage lenders all compete with the traditional building societies to lend money in the mortgage market. Mortgage money is in plentiful supply and building societies are wholly commercial organisations. Today mortgage money is simply another commodity.

The importance of shopping around to obtain the most competitive mortgage rate is explained in detail in Chapter 4.

UNDERSTANDING THE ROLE OF THE SURVEYOR

The surveyor's role is often widely misunderstood. Many people mistakenly believe that the survey will point out any defects that the property has and confirm its market value. The surveyor will not do this unless they are paid an additional fee to do so.

About 80 per cent of all house buyers opt for the most basic form of survey, the **mortgage valuation**. This is exactly what it says it is. The surveyor acts for his client, ie the mortgage lender, and answers just one question: is the property satisfactory security for the loan that is being advanced?

If you want to know more about the condition of the property, you will need to instruct the surveyor to undertake a home buyer's report or a building survey. The pros and cons of the different types of survey are explained in detail in Chapter 9.

UNDERSTANDING THE ROLE OF YOUR SOLICITOR

Your solicitor's job is to safeguard your legal interest and the interests of your mortgage lender (if any). Their main functions are as follows.

Receiving/negotiating the draft contract

Your solicitor will check the contract prepared by the vendor's solicitors and amend any clauses which may be detrimental to your interests.

Sending a local search to the council

A local authority search verifies, amongst other things, whether the road is private (in which case you may have to pay for its maintenance), whether the property could be affected by any road widening schemes and whether the property is in a conservation area. Some local authorities take several weeks to deal with search enquiries and it is therefore important to apply for the search as soon as the sale has been agreed.

Sending preliminary enquiries to the vendor's solicitor

This is a list of questions about the property. It will include questions such as 'Does the property have mains drainage?' and 'Have there been any disputes over boundaries and fences?' Most of the questions are fairly standard and most solicitors use a standard word processed form with supplementary questions added as necessary.

Checking the mortgage offer

Before exchanging contracts your solicitor will check that your mortgage offer is in order and that you are able to comply with all its terms and conditions.

Arranging signing of the contract

Once your solicitor is happy with the terms of the contract you will be asked to sign it. At this point the solicitor will need your deposit (usually 10 per cent of the purchase price).

Exchanging contracts

Your solicitor should not exchange contracts until he or she is happy with the terms of the contract, the results of the searches and that your mortgage and other funding is in place. Once you have exchanged contracts the sale is binding. If you withdraw now, you will forfeit your deposit. The vendor may also sue you for additional damages.

Checking the vendor's title

The vendor's solicitor will have sent your solicitor proof of the title in the form of a copy of the title deeds or a summary of their contents (known as an 'abstract title'). If your solicitor has any questions, he will ask for clarification in writing. This correspondence is known as 'requisitions on title'.

Checking mortgage arrangements

Your solicitor will inform your mortgage lender of the completion date and ask them to ensure that the necessary mortgage funds are available on that date. He will also arrange for you to sign the mortgage deed and the conveyance or transfer document (see next paragraph).

Preparing draft conveyance or transfer

Your solicitor will prepare a draft transfer if the land is registered, or a conveyance if the land is unregistered (see later). This is the deed which will pass the vendor's interest in the property to you. This draft conveyance or transfer will then be sent to the vendor's solicitor to check that it is in accordance with the terms of the contract.

Arranging signing of final documents

These will include the final (known as the engrossed) version of the conveyance or transfer and the mortgage deed. You will also at this time need to give your solicitor a cheque for the balance of any purchase monies required which are not to be paid out of your mortgage advance.

Commissioning final searches

Your solicitor will carry out two final searches before completion. A bankruptcy search will confirm that the vendor is not bankrupt. If they are, the property might no longer be theirs to sell. The second and final search is a land charges search. This will ensure that there are no undisclosed mortgages or other charges against the property.

Arranging payment of Stamp Duty

If the purchase price was more than £120,000, the conveyance or transfer has to be sent to the Inland Revenue. A tax known as Stamp Duty is payable on all transactions over £120,000 according to the following scale:

◆　£120,001 – £250,000: Stamp Duty payable at 1 per cent
◆　£250,001 – £500,000: Stamp Duty payable at 3 per cent
◆　£500,001 and above: Stamp Duty payable at 4 per cent.

Arranging registration of title

Your solicitor's penultimate job is to register your title with the Land Registry. If you bought the property in joint names, all owners will be registered in the Proprietorship Register. Details of your mortgage and other charges will also be included in the Charges Register.

Dealing with the Charge Certificate

Once your title has been registered, the Land Registry will send a Charge Certificate to your solicitor. This confirms that the Land Registry has recorded the charge against the property. Your solicitor will forward the Charge Certificate to your mortgage lender.

If no mortgage is involved, the Land Registry will send your solicitor a Land Certificate. This proves that you own the property outright. It is an extremely important document and it is important to keep it in a safe place (most people entrust it to their bank).

UNDERSTANDING THE ROLE OF THE VENDOR'S SOLICITOR

The vendor's solicitor is on the vendor's side. Their job is to provide your solicitor with the information that is requested and to protect their client's legal interests during the course of the sale. Their main functions during the sale are as follows.

Obtaining the title deeds

The title deeds are the documents (electronic or hard copy) that prove that the vendor actually owns the property that he is selling to you. If the property is mortgaged, they will usually be held by the mortgagee. In most cases obtaining the title deeds will take seven to ten days.

Ordering office copy entries

If the property is registered (see later), the vendor's solicitor will apply to the Land Registry for office copy entries of the title. The office copy entries prove that the property is registered. They also give details of mortgages or other charges secured on the property and include a plan showing the extent of the land that is being sold.

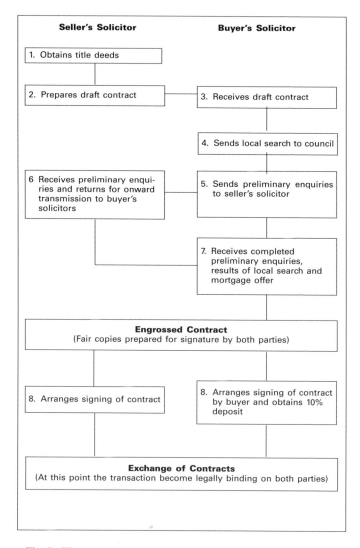

Seller's Solicitor   **Buyer's Solicitor**

1. Obtains title deeds

2. Prepares draft contract

3. Receives draft contract

4. Sends local search to council

6 Receives preliminary enquiries and returns for onward
transmission to buyer's
solicitors

5. Sends preliminary enquiries
to seller's solicitor

7. Receives completed
preliminary enquiries,
results of local search and
mortgage offer

Engrossed Contract
(Fair copies prepared for signature by both parties)

8. Arranges signing of contract

8. Arranges signing of contract
by buyer and obtains 10%
deposit

Exchange of Contracts
(At this point the transaction become legally binding on both parties)

Fig. 2. The conveyancing process involving your own and the
vendor's solicitor.

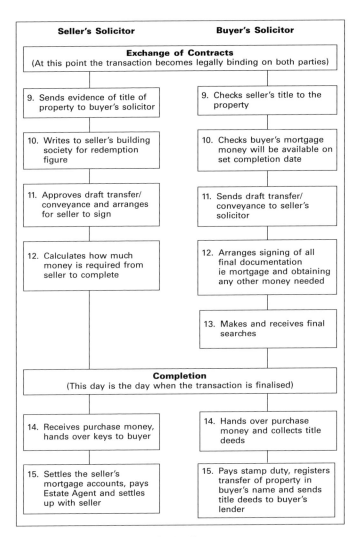

Seller's Solicitor	Buyer's Solicitor
Exchange of Contracts (At this point the transaction becomes legally binding on both parties)	
9. Sends evidence of title of property to buyer's solicitor	9. Checks seller's title to the property
10. Writes to seller's building society for redemption figure	10. Checks buyer's mortgage money will be available on set completion date
11. Approves draft transfer/conveyance and arranges for seller to sign	11. Sends draft transfer/conveyance to seller's solicitor
12. Calculates how much money is required from seller to complete	12. Arranges signing of all final documentation ie mortgage and obtaining any other money needed
	13. Makes and receives final searches
Completion (This day is the day when the transaction is finalised)	
14. Receives purchase money, hands over keys to buyer	14. Hands over purchase money and collects title deeds
15. Settles the seller's mortgage accounts, pays Estate Agent and settles up with seller	15. Pays stamp duty, registers transfer of property in buyer's name and sends title deeds to buyer's lender

Fig. 2. Cont.

(Used by kind permission of the National Association of Estate Agents and the Residential Estate Agency Training and Education Association.)

If the property is 'unregistered' (see later) a Public Index Map Search is carried out to obtain proof of ownership.

Preparing the draft contract

This is the document that sets out all the terms of the sale. It will be sent to your solicitor for approval.

Answering preliminary enquiries

Your solicitor will ask a number of questions about the property, such as 'Is the property connected to mains drainage?' and 'Have there ever been any disputes over boundaries or fences?' The vendor's solicitor is obliged to answer these questions truthfully. However, in practice many of the answers will be qualified with phrases such as 'As far as the seller is aware', or 'To the best of our knowledge.'

Preparing engrossed contract

This is the final version of the contract which will be signed by both parties.

Arranging for the vendor to sign the contract

If the property is jointly owned, all parties will need to sign.

Receiving the deposit on exchange of contracts

This is usually 10 per cent of the purchase price but a lesser figure is sometimes negotiated. Once contracts have been exchanged, the sale becomes binding on both parties and failure to complete could lead to the forfeiture of this deposit.

Sending evidence of title to the purchaser's solicitor

Once contracts have been exchanged, the vendor's solicitor will send your solicitor a copy of the deeds or a summary of their contents (known as an abstract of title).

Discharging mortgages

The vendor's solicitor will ask the vendor's building society for a final settlement and ensure that the mortgage is paid out of the proceeds of the sale.

Arranging signing of final documents

The vendor's solicitor will check that the transfer or conveyance (see later) is in accordance with the terms of the contract before the vendor signs the final documents.

Arranging completion

The vendor's solicitor will receive the balance of the purchase monies and in return will hand over the title deeds to your solicitor.

Arranging the removal of charges

If the vendor had a mortgage on the property, this will be registered at the Land Registry. If this is the case, the vendor's solicitor must deduct the sum owing from the proceeds of the sale and send it, together with the mortgage form (known as Form 53) to the mortgage lender. The mortgage lender will officially stamp the form to confirm that the mortgage has been paid and return it to the vendor's solicitors. The latter will forward the form to your solicitor who will forward it to the Land Registry.

BUYING A PROPERTY WITH UNREGISTERED TITLE

There are two systems of land conveyancing in England and Wales:

◆ registered title
◆ and unregistered title.

In the first case the title to the land is registered at the Land Registry and guaranteed by the state. Disputes over title are therefore extremely rare.

In the unregistered system title must be proved by checking back through details of previous conveyances. Where land is unregistered, disputes over title are much more common and can take a considerable time to resolve.

One day all land in England and Wales will be registered. In the meanwhile, if you find that the property that you are buying does not have registered title you should be prepared to allow extra time for the conveyancing process to be completed. You will also probably find that the conveyancing costs are significantly higher.

BUYING A LEASEHOLD PROPERTY

◆ A **freehold** property is yours forever.

◆ A **leasehold** property is owned by a 'freeholder' who grants you the right to live there for a certain period of time.

Most new leases are for a duration of 99 or sometimes 999 years, although in some areas – particularly central London

– they are often much shorter. The pros and cons of buying a leasehold property are discussed in Chapter 5.

If you do decide to buy a leasehold property, your solicitor will have to make two further checks.

Checking the terms of the lease

The lease is a lengthy document that sets out, amongst other things, who is responsible for maintaining the building and any restrictions that are imposed on the owners (for example, not to keep a petanimal). Your solicitor will read the lease carefully to check that it does not contain any clauses that are detrimental to your interests. Some of the problems that are found with leases are explained in Chapter 11.

Checking that service charges and ground rents have been paid

The service charge reflects each leaseholder's share of the cost of maintaining the building. The ground rent is a (usually) small rent that the leaseholder must pay to the freeholder for the whole duration of the lease. Failure to pay service charges and ground rent on time can result in the forfeiture of the lease, so your solicitor will check carefully that all payments are up to date.

BUYING A PROPERTY IN SCOTLAND

The procedure for buying a property in Scotland is entirely different. Under the Scottish system the seller invites offers and a legally binding contract is created as soon as an offer is accepted. In an active market a closing date is usually set for offers.

On or before the closing date the purchaser's solicitor sends a detailed offer to the vendor's solicitor. This will include the price offered, the date when possession is required and any special conditions (for example, subject to survey). There will also be conditions that the vendor's solicitor must provide proof of title and clear searches.

Once the offer has been accepted, letters are exchanged between the solicitors in order to clear up all outstanding matters. These letters are known as 'missives'. Once both parties are satisfied, the contract is made unconditional – the English equivalent of exchange of contracts. The procedures after contracts have been exchanged are broadly similar to those that apply in England.

The Scottish system is quicker than the English one but it does have several drawbacks. The main ones are explained below.

Wasted costs

Would-be buyers often have to spend quite a lot of money on valuation and survey fees before they can make an offer for a property. If their offer is refused, this money will have been wasted. Many buyers incur abortive survey fees several times before they manage to buy a property.

Coordinating the chain

Under the Scottish system it is much harder for buyers to coordinate their house purchase with their house sale. The consequence of this is that Scottish buyers have to arrange bridging finance and/or arrange temporary accommodation far more often than their English counterparts.

HOME BUYING IN THE FUTURE

From 2007 it will become an offence to market a property without first preparing a home information pack. This will have to be put together by the seller *before* they put their property onto the market. It is likely that the home information pack will include:

◆ Copies of title documents
◆ Replies to standard preliminary enquiries made on behalf of buyers.
◆ Replies to local authority searches.
◆ Copies of any planning, listed building and building regulation consents.
◆ For new properties, copies of warranties and guarantees.
◆ Any guarantees for work carried out on the property.
◆ A surveyor's report on the condition of the property.
◆ A draft contract.

For leasehold properties the information pack would also include:

◆ A copy of the lease.
◆ Accounts and receipts for service charges.
◆ Building insurance policy and receipts for premiums.
◆ Regulations made by the landlord or management company.
◆ The landlord or management company's memorandum and articles.

The proposed new home buying process should bring important benefits for the consumer. By making more information available at the outset average transaction times could be speeded up considerably and the fall-through rate significantly reduced. The implications of this are discussed during later chapters.

Selling Your Current Property

This chapter deals with selling your current property. If you are buying for the first time go straight to Chapter 4.

About 80 per cent of all house buyers have to sell their existing property before they buy their next one.

If the purchase of your next property is dependent on the sale of your current one, you really do need to sell before you start looking seriously.

Trying to do things the other way round will almost certainly lead to frustration, disappointment and unnecessary expense.

WHY YOU MUST SELL BEFORE YOU BUY

◆ If you try to buy your next property before you have secured an offer on your current one, you will be disadvantaged at both ends of the transaction.

◆ Many vendors will reject your offer out of hand if you are not in a position to proceed with your purchase immediately. It is extremely frustrating to find your dream house and then be told that you cannot have it.

◆ Even if you do manage to persuade a vendor to accept your offer, your poor buying position might well mean that you have to pay over the odds for the property.

◆ When it comes to selling your current property you will also be at a disadvantage because you will need to sell quickly in order to avoid losing the property that you are trying to buy. This could mean that you are not able to hold out for the best price for the property that you are selling.

Increasing the risks

The risk of the purchase falling through is also greatly increased. If you are not in a position to proceed immediately your vendor might well decide to keep the property on the market in case you are not able to sell yours within a reasonable period of time. If someone else in a better buying position makes an offer for the property, there is a high risk that your vendor will choose to accept it. This could leave you with a bill for abortive legal fees and survey fees of several hundred pounds.

Perhaps the worst risk of all, though, is that your determination to secure the house of your dreams might make you act irrationally. Buyers can become so determined to secure a property that they end up taking out ruinously expensive bridging loans. There are very few cases where this can be justified.

CASE STUDIES
Sue and Steven start looking too soon

Sue and Steven O wanted to move from a three-bedroomed semi to a four-bedroomed detached house in Guildford, Surrey. They were aware that they ought to sell their current property first but decided to view a few properties just to see what they could get for their money. The very first house that they saw was absolutely perfect. It had everything they had ever wanted and a fabulous landscaped garden looking out over open fields. They were convinced that they would never find another house quite like it.

Much against their better judgement they put an offer in for five per cent less than the asking price. The vendor rejected it out of hand and said that if they wanted her to wait until they had sold their own property she would require the full asking price.

Steve and Sue were determined to have the property so they agreed to offer the full asking price. They immediately put their own property up for sale at £10,000 less than the estate agent's recommended figure, in order to achieve a quick sale. They also applied for a mortgage on the new property and instructed solicitors to start work.

Three weeks later they heard their vendor had received an offer from someone who could proceed immediately, and that she had decided to take it. They had still not received an offer on their current property and, try as they might, Steve and Sue could not persuade their vendor to wait any longer.

Commenting on her experience six months later, Sue says 'I wish we had never seen the original property. Apart from the stress and frustration, we ended up with a bill for abortive legal fees, and survey fees of more than £400, and probably sold our current property for less than it was worth (it is very difficult to increase an asking price). The final irony, though, is that the house we did eventually buy is much nicer than the one we lost. Next time we will be sure to sell first.'

Robin counts the cost of a bridging loan

Robin C bought a delightful house in Chelsea in the summer of 1998. He had not sold his current flat but it was a very popular area and he felt confident that it would sell quickly. Furthermore the house that he was buying was for sale at such an attractive price that he felt able to justify the cost of a bridging loan.

When Robin had not bargained for was the weakening of the London property market which occurred in the second half of 1998. His flat remained unsold for six months and the cost of the open bridging loan was crippling. Eventually he sold his flat in January 1999 for 15 per cent less than the original asking price.

Commenting on his experience, Robin says, 'With

hindsight buying the house before I sold the flat was a bad decision. Although the house seemed a bargain, the cost of the bridging loan has swallowed up all my paper profit and has left me so short of funds that I have not even be able to furnish the new house property.'

ACCEPTING A CONDITIONAL OFFER ON YOUR PROPERTY

If you take the advice to sell first, you need to guard against the risk of not being able to find suitable property to buy within a reasonable period of time. You will also need to guard against the risk of underselling your property.

Selling in a rising market

In a buoyant market there can be periods when property values are rising at the rate of two or even three per cent per month. If you fix the sale price of your current property then take two or three months to find somewhere to buy, you could find yourself at a considerable disadvantage. In a rapidly rising market it is often best to accept an offer subject to being able to find a suitable property to buy within a given period (say four weeks). If you are not able to find a property within the period it may be necessary to renegotiate the sale price agreed with your own buyer.

Selling in a falling market

In a falling market the opposite holds true. If you are not able to find a property quickly your buyer may want to renegotiate the price downwards. However, if you are buying another property yourself you will probably have the compensation of being able to buy your next property at a correspondingly lower price.

Accepting conditionally

The thing to remember throughout is that no one can make you move out of your current property unless you want to. If you really can't find a suitable property to buy, the worst that can happen is that you have to tell your would-be purchasers that you are no longer able to sell them your property.

Whilst you always have this option, it would not be fair to make promises that you know to be false or to cause your would-be purchaser unnecessary cost or inconvenience. The best way to achieve this is to make it clear that acceptance of their offer is subject to being able to find a suitable property to buy. If you have serious doubts about being able to find somewhere suitable, it may also be as well to discourage your purchaser from proceeding with their mortgage application or conveyancing work until you have found somewhere. This will keep both sides' abortive costs to a minimum in the event that the sale does not proceed.

WHAT TO DO IF YOU CAN'T FIND A PROPERTY

If you really can't find a property, don't panic and above all don't buy any old house just to appease your purchaser. A home is far too important a purchase to compromise over and, if you buy the wrong property in a hurry, you might end up having to move again.

If you really can't find a property within the agreed timescale, you will have to decide between one of three options.

Moving into temporary accommodation

There is a plentiful supply of high quality rented accommodation in most areas of the country (see Chapter 1). Moving twice is inconvenient but your new status as a buyer who can proceed immediately will put you in a very strong negotiating position. Your reward for spending six months in rented accommodation might be the chance to buy a much better property at a much better price.

Negotiating an extension

If you explain the situation truthfully to your buyers, you may be able to persuade them to wait a little longer. For the reasons explained earlier in this chapter, it may be necessary to renegotiate some of the other terms of the sale as well as the timescale.

Withdrawing from the sale

The final option is to withdraw from the sale. Your buyers may be angry and disappointed, but better this than spending the next 20 years in a house that you don't really like.

IF YOU MUST BUY FIRST

If you really must buy first there is a high probability that you will end up facing the choice between losing the property that you are trying to buy or taking out a bridging loan.

> The best advice is nearly always to let your dream house go.

As the old saying goes 'Houses are like buses, another one will always come along eventually.'

If you are determined to proceed with your purchase you will probably need to arrange a bridging loan. There are two different types of bridging loan:

◆ a 'closed loan'
◆ and an 'open loan'.

Closed loans

A closed loan is a loan that is made for a set period of time. This type of loan is designed for the situation where you have exchanged contracts on both your purchase and your sale but need money to complete on your purchase before you receive the proceeds from your sale. This type of loan is relatively low risk for the lender and closed bridging loans are reasonably easy to obtain.

The best place to obtain such a loan is often your current or new mortgage lender or your own bank. Despite the relatively low risk, closed bridging loan finance is still expensive. Another drawback is that the interest must be paid on a monthly basis – it is not usually possible to add it to your mortgage.

Open loans

If you have not even exchanged contracts on your sale, you will need an open bridging loan, ie a loan for an unspecified period of time. This type of loan is much riskier for the lender. You might never be able to sell your current property and go bankrupt under the strain of paying two loans. Because of this, open bridging loans are much harder to obtain and much more expensive. There are a number of specialist lenders operating in this market but the best place to start may again be your current mortgage lender or your bank.

Lending in the future

It is to be hoped that in the future lenders will develop specialised bridging loans that are both more affordable and easier to obtain. The ideal would be to allow the cost of a closed bridging loan to be added to the mortgage on the next property and repaid over the entire period of the next loan.

$$\left(4 \right)$$

Financing the Purchase

Your mortgage will probably be the biggest financial commitment that you will ever make. This chapter will show you how to choose the right loan from the thousands of options that are available.

Getting your loan sorted out before you start looking seriously will put you in a better position to buy and save a lot of time later.

DISCOVERING IF YOU ARE CREDITWORTHY

If you are deemed to be 'uncreditworthy' your choice of mortgage lender will be severely restricted. Indeed, it may not be possible to borrow money at all. Mortgage lenders will determine whether you are creditworthy in one of three ways.

Credit scoring

Credit scoring is the process by which a mortgage lender looks back at all its previous cases and tries to identify the factors that make people statistically more likely to default on their loans. It then designs a process in which points are deducted if certain features apply to them.

For example, the lenders' research might show that people who are self-employed are statistically twice as likely to default on their loans as people who are employed. Accordingly self-employed applicants would lose 20 marks from their credit score. Further research might show that people who are less than 25 years old are statistically three times more likely to default on their loans than older people. Accordingly applicants who are less than 25 years would lose 30 marks from their credit score.

Point-scoring

Each mortgage lender has its own credit scoring process and each deducts marks for different criteria. However, generally speaking you will lose points if you:

◆ are self-employed;
◆ have changed jobs recently;
◆ have an unstable employment record (ie you have changed jobs frequently)
◆ have moved home recently or often;
◆ are not on the electoral register;
◆ have never had a mortgage or any other loan;
◆ are single or cohabiting with a partner.

If your total credit score falls below a certain level, the lender will decline your mortgage application.

Credit scoring is a crude and sometimes unfair process. From time to time stories appear in the press about someone who earns a million pounds a year but was refused a small mortgage because he has just changed his job and moved house. But despite these occasional glitches, credit scoring is a cheap and, statistically speaking, fairly accurate way to assess how likely an applicant is to default on their mortgage payments and it seems likely that most mortgage lenders will continue to use it.

Using a mortgage broker
A good mortgage broker should be able to warn you about whether your personal circumstances make you likely to fail a credit scoring test. They should advise you on what action to take to avoid your application being rejected.

Asking for financial references
In addition to 'credit scoring' your application, the mortgage lender will also take up financial references. These will include:

◆ A search to make sure that you have never been declared bankrupt.
◆ A search to make sure that you do not have any County Court Judgements for debt (CCJs).
◆ A search to make sure that payments due on any previous loans have been made on time.

This information is available to lenders 'on line' from any of the country's credit reference agencies.

County Court Judgements
By far the greatest number of problems with financial references occur because of County Court Judgements for debt. Many thousands of people have County Court Judgements for debt registered against them of which they are completely unaware: the cause of the problem is the ease

with which a County Court Judgement for debt can be obtained.

If you have a County Court Judgement for debt registered against you, your choice of mortgage lender will be severely restricted. If you have just one County Court Judgement for debt and you disclose it on the mortgage application, and the sum involved is relatively small (usually less than about £2,000) and the debt has been 'satisfied' (ie repaid in full), then it may still be possible to obtain a loan with a mainstream mortgage lender.

If you have more than one County Court Judgement against you or if the sum involved is more than about £2,000, or if the debt is still partly or wholly outstanding or you did not disclose it on the mortgage application form (even if you did not know of its existence), your mortgage application will normally be refused.

Using a specialist lender
In such cases your only option will be to apply to a mortgage lender who specialises in 'credit impaired' cases. The interest rate charged on such a loan will almost certainly be much higher than that charged by the mainstream lenders and such a mortgage should be considered only as a last resort.

Requiring employment references
The final check that the mortgage lender will make is to take up references from your employer. To avoid problems and delays you need to ensure that your employer responds to the reference request immediately, and that they complete

the lender's official form rather than just sending the information in letter form.

DECIDING HOW MUCH YOU CAN BORROW

Most mortgage lenders will lend a maximum of four times your income plus once the income of your spouse. On this basis a couple earning £20,000 and £10,000 respectively would be able to borrow £20,000 × 4 = £80,000 plus £10,000 × 1 = £10,000, ie a total of £90,000. These limits may seem over-cautious. They are not. They are sensible limits designed to prevent borrowers from over-stretching themselves.

A young couple who are both in secure employment may feel confident enough to borrow far more than this. However, they have no way of knowing what the future may bring.

◆ Interest rates might rise, causing their mortgage payments to increase enormously.

◆ An unplanned pregnancy might require one partner to give up work sooner than they had planned.

◆ Redundancy or illness could reduce the family's income without warning.

The risk of mortgaging yourself up to the hilt might be justified if:

◆ You have good reason to believe that your income will rise rapidly in the future.

◆ You are confident about the security of your employment.

◆ You have insurance to protect your income in the event of redundancy or illness.

◆ You have protected against the risk of interest rates rising by taking out a fixed rate mortgage (see later).

In all other cases it may be safer to stick to the borrowing limits imposed by the mainstream mortgage lenders.

Treatment of overtime and commission payments

A great deal of confusion is caused by the way that mortgage lenders treat overtime and commission payments. If your employer states that overtime or commission is 'guaranteed' most lenders will treat it as if it were basic salary. If it is not guaranteed, most mortgage lenders will only allow half its value when calculating how much you can afford to borrow.

For example:

Miss A earns £10,000 basic salary plus £10,000 guaranteed commission. She can borrow 4 × £10,000 plus 4 × £10,000, ie £80,000.

Miss B earns £10,000 basic salary and £10,000 non-guaranteed commission. She can borrow 4 × £10,000 plus 2 × £10,000, ie £60,000.

If any part of your salary is paid by way of overtime or commission, you need to check with your employer whether this will be described as guaranteed or non-guaranteed before you apply for a mortgage.

Self-employed applicants

Most of the mainstream lenders require self-employed applicants to provide three years' audited accounts to confirm their income. If you cannot do so your choice of mortgage lender will be restricted.

Non-status mortgages

If you have recently become self-employed, or if you cannot prove your income, you really need to speak to a specialist mortgage broker in order to determine what options are available. Many self-employed applicants end up taking a 'non-status' mortgage. This means that the mortgage lender relies on the value of the property for their security rather than on the income of the applicant. Non-status loans are normally limited to a maximum of 75 per cent of the value of the property (ie you will need to be able to find a deposit of at least £25,000 to buy a £100,000 property).

Maximum loans as a percentage of the property's value

Few mortgage lenders will lend more than 95 per cent of the property's value. This means you will have to find a deposit of £5,000 in order to purchase a £100,000 property. Some lenders will lend 100 per cent of the purchase price, but because they perceive a 100 per cent mortgage as being higher risk the cost of borrowing will usually be higher.

The opposite is also true. If you need to borrow less than about 75 per cent of the value of the property that you are buying, you may be able to get a lower interest rate which reflects the lower risk to the lender.

Working out negative equity problems

Some lenders will lend more than 100 per cent of the purchase price of the property. However, such loans are normally restricted to people who are in negative equity (ie they own a property which is worth less than the mortgage outstanding on it). If you are in such a position you need to seek the advice of a specialist mortgage broker regarding the options that are open to you.

Indemnity guarantee premiums

If you need to borrow more than a certain percentage of the purchase price, you may need to pay a **mortgage indemnity** guarantee premium. The 'trigger point' varies from lender to lender but is usually around 75 to 80 per cent.

Indemnity insurance protects the building society *but not you* against the risk of losing money if you default on your mortgage and the property is resold for less than the outstanding mortgage.

Indemnity guarantee premium rates vary considerably from lender to lender so it pays to shop around. Some will allow the premium to be added to the loan. Some insist that it is paid in cash. Some lenders have stopped charging for indemnity insurance altogether although the cost may be recouped elsewhere in the loan.

UNDERSTANDING THE ROLE OF THE MORTGAGE BROKER

Approximately 40 per cent of all mortgages are still arranged directly with a mortgage lender rather than through a mortgage broker. This is astonishing. If you walk into a bank or building society and say 'I'd like a mortgage please' you will only be told about the mortgage products that are available through that bank or building society. They are certainly not going to say that another building society is offering a much better rate.

Approximately 150 mortgage providers compete for customers in the UK mortgage market. Most of these 150 providers offer a variety of different types of mortgage schemes (see later) and this means that there are literally thousands of different mortgage options to choose from. The chance of finding the mortgage that is best for you by walking into a bank or building society at random is at least 150 to one against..

Before you choose a mortgage, speak to a mortgage broker. A good one will look across the whole mortgage market and advise on which is best for you.

Finding a mortgage broker

Most mortgage brokers fall into one of four categories:

◆ Independent mortgage brokers – look in *Yellow Pages* under Mortgage Brokers.

◆ Independent financial advisers – look in *Yellow Pages* under Financial Advisers. Before making an appointment, check that the firm specialises in the mortgage market.

◆ Solicitors – some solicitors have a financial services division. Check that the person you see specialises in the mortgage market before you make an appointment.

◆ Estate agents – most estate agents have an in-house mortgage broker. It is not necessary to buy a house from an estate agent in order to use their mortgage broker. Most will be delighted to arrange a mortgage for you even if you are buying a house from one of their competitors.

CHOOSING A MORTGAGE BROKER

Choosing the right mortgage broker could save you many thousands of pounds over the full mortgage term, and a great deal of time and frustration in the shorter term. It is therefore well worth taking some care over your choice. Here are some questions that you can ask that will help you to make the right choice.

◆ Are you able to advise me on the mortgage products that are available from all the 150 UK mortgage lenders? If not, how many mortgage lenders do you have access to?

◆ Do you have access to mortgage sourcing software, ie a computer programme that will give up-to-date advice on the latest schemes that are available and help you to assess which one is the best for me?

◆ How many different lenders did you deal with last year? The answer should be at least a dozen.

◆ What percentage of all your mortgage lending do you refer to the top four leaders? Some brokers place most of their lending with just three or four lenders and in return receive an enhanced level of commission known as a procuration fee.

◆ How long have you been a financial adviser?

◆ Approximately how many mortgages did you (and/or your firm) arrange last year? Some financial advisers specialise in other areas such as pensions and arrange very few mortgages. Such advisers are unlikely to have the experience necessary to advise you on the best mortgage scheme.

◆ What professional qualifications do you have?

◆ Are you an independent financial adviser or an appointed representative of just one life assurance company? In an ideal world you would want to deal with an independent financial adviser who specialises in the mortgage market. However, such firms are few and far between. If you have to compromise, it is usually better to choose a broker who specialises in the mortgage market and is an appointed representative of a well-known insurance company rather than an independent financial adviser who knows little about the mortgage market.

◆ How will you charge me for your work? Most brokers will be paid a commission for selling you an insurance policy. They often also receive a smaller commission from the mortgage lender. Some brokers also charge an arrangement fee. This is particularly common when the commission that can be earned is small. Some brokers, particularly IFAs, have a policy of refunding all commissions to the client and charging for their advice on an hourly basis. They believe that this helps to ensure impartiality.

◆ Why should I arrange my mortgage through you?

Before you make a final decision you should try to see two or three brokers and ask these questions of each of them. The time to do this is when you first start looking for a property. Do not wait until you have found somewhere. Choosing a mortgage is a decision that is too important to make under pressure.

The majority of mortgage brokers will be happy to spend half an hour with you describing their service without charge and without obligation. Those who are not are not worth dealing with.

CHOOSING A LENDING SOURCE

Before making a recommendation a good broker will consider many different criteria.

Type of lending scheme required

The two most common options are:

◆ variable rate
◆ and fixed rate.

Variable rate mortgages
The interest rate charged on a variable rate mortgage will fluctuate in line with the base rate set by the Bank of England. In January 1999 the cost of a variable rate mortgage was around seven-and-a-half per cent. However, mortgage rates in the past have been as high as 18 per cent. Interest rates could rise to this level again. Just imagine the consequences if they were to do so. Someone currently making mortgage payments of £750 per month would have

to pay £1,800 per month. Where would they find the other £1,050 per month from? The consequence could be the loss of their home.

Fixed rate mortgages

The main alternative is a fixed rate mortgage. As the name implies, the interest rate is fixed for an agreed period. This could be anywhere from one to 25 years. If interest rates rose during this period, you would be the winner. If they fell, you would end up paying more than you needed to for your mortgage.

For example:

> Mr A fixes at seven per cent for one year and makes payments of £7,000 per annum or £583.33 per month.
> Interest rates rise immediately to ten per cent.
> Payments would have been £10,000 per annum or £833.33 per month.
> Mr A, however, continues to pay £583.33.
> By the end of the year he has saved three per cent, ie £3,000.

> (This is a simplified example. Due to the way that interest rates are calculated the real interest payments would be a little different to this.)

A lot of people try to out-guess the markets. This is not the right reason to take out a fixed rate loan. A fixed rate loan gives you the security that your mortgage payments will not rise for a given period. If interest rates fall, the saving that you could have made becomes the price that you paid for that security. If interest rates rise during the period of the fix you have got a bonus.

The question to ask yourself therefore is for what period, if any, you need the security of a fixed rate mortgage.

◆ You may want to fix for the whole mortgage term.
◆ You may want to fix for just the first three to five years, ie the period when the burden of paying a new mortgage will be heaviest.
◆ If you can comfortably afford the repayments, you may not want to fix at all.

Choosing which scheme

A good mortgage broker will advice you on whether to take a fixed or variable rate mortgage and what period to fix for. If you decide on, say, a five-year fix, the broker will compile a list of mortgage providers who offer competitive rates for a five-year fixed term.

Constraints imposed by each lender's lending criteria

Each of the mortgage lenders have their own quirks about the type of property on which they will lend. These are mostly based on any bad experiences that they have had with loans which have gone wrong in the past.

Examples of the type of property that some mortgage lenders will not lend on would include:

◆ property built before 1919
◆ property that is above commercial premises
◆ any property with a thatched roof
◆ any property worth more than a certain value
◆ any property outside a certain geographical area.

Your mortgage broker will check that the property which you are buying meets the lending criteria of your proposed lender. If you are buying an unusual property you may find that your choice of mortgage lender is severely restricted.

Constraints imposed by your personal or financial circumstances

As I explained earlier in this chapter your choice of mortgage lender will be severely restricted if you are self-employed, if you have any County Court Judgements for debt or if you want to borrow more than four times your salary.

Current interest rate

Having compiled a short list of possible lenders, the broker should go on to compare the interest rate that is currently being charged by each. Interest rates vary hugely between different mortgage lenders. The additional cost over the term of the loan can be enormous. For example, on a £50,000 mortgage a one per cent increase in the interest rate paid would mean extra payments of:

◆ £42 per month
◆ £500 per year
◆ £12,500 over the full term of the loan.

In January 2005, the current interest rates charged by different mortgage lenders varied by nearly 5%. This would mean extra payments over 25 years of £62,500 on a £50,000 loan! This example is an extreme one but shows how important it is to shop around.

Historic interest rates

It is important to remember that a mortgage is a 25-year commitment. It would be a grave mistake to choose a mortgage lender who is offering a cheap interest rate now but puts it up as soon as you have taken out your loan. A good mortgage broker will be able to advise you on which mortgage lenders have offered consistently competitive mortgage rates.

Discounts/cash/free insurance/waiver of fees

The mortgage market is fiercely competitive and many mortgage lenders try to attract new borrowers by offering various discounts and other incentives. Most of these take one of four forms.

Discounts

The lender may offer a discount of, say, five per cent for the first year. This means that instead of paying say eight per cent you pay only three per cent. This can be tremendously useful if you have spent all your money on new furniture, carpets and curtains.

Cash-backs

Another way of giving a discount is a cash-back. This means that on completion you will receive an agreed sum back in cash. This is another way to fund the cost of furnishing and redecorating a new property.

Free insurances

A third way of giving a discount is through free insurances. For example, the lender may say that it will pay the premiums for buildings insurance for the first five years.

Waiver of fees

The fourth way of giving a discount is for the lender to waive the cost of the survey fee and/or the arrangement fee.

Some lenders offer a package of incentives that includes a combination of all of the above.

Trying to calculate whether a five per cent discount for the first years is worth more than no survey fee and free buildings insurance for the next five years is extremely difficult. In fact, the calculations are so complex that even the mortgage broker will probably use a computer programme in order to determine which package offers the best value.

Special conditions

The next criterion that the broker will consider is whether the proposed mortgage lender has imposed any special conditions on the loan. These often onerous conditions are sometimes buried in the small print. Two of the most common are redemption penalties and compulsory insurances.

Redemption penalties

If you repay the mortgage within, for instance, the first five years, you might be liable to pay a redemption penalty. This can be one, three, six, nine or even 12 months' interest. Your broker's job is to draw your attention to all such conditions. If you are planning to move again within the redemption period your broker may advise you to choose a different mortgage lender.

Compulsory insurances

The second common trick is to insist that you take the lender's buildings or contents insurance for the whole of the mortgage term. The cost of the policy is often far more than that of a similar policy elsewhere. If this is the case, your broker may advise you to consider an alternative mortgage lender.

Speed and efficiency of services

The average time taken to process a mortgage application varies hugely between different mortgage lenders and even between different branches of the same mortgage lender. The most efficient regularly process applications in less than ten working days. The least efficient often take six to eight weeks.

Every extra day that you are waiting for a mortgage offer is an extra day when something can go wrong. It is therefore essential to choose a mortgage lender with a reputation for efficiency. Your broker will be able to advise you on which lenders meet this criterion.

After sales service

Some mortgage lenders have a reputation for poor after sales service and inefficient administration. An example of such inefficiency would be a lender which 'forgets' to collect the mortgage payments by direct debit for several months and then takes all the payments in one go. Dealing with the consequences of such maladministration can be very stressful and time consuming. Your broker should be able to steer you away from lenders with a particularly poor reputation for after sales service.

Summary

There are at least 2,000 alternative mortgage options and at least eight different criteria to consider - a total of at least 16,000 pieces of information to consider. From this it should be clear that an informed choice can only be made after speaking to a professional.

CASE STUDY
Carl does not shop around

Carl B bought a brand new three-bedroomed detached property for £75,000. On the advice of his father he arranged a mortgage through the ABC Building Society without shopping around. Two months later whilst chatting to his new neighbour, Carl discovered that he was paying £60 per month more for his mortgage than he need have done.

Commenting on his experience Carl says, 'I had no idea that mortgage rates varied so much. Next time I will shop around more carefully.'

CHOOSING A REPAYMENT METHOD

Once you have decided on a lending source, you need to decide how you are going to repay the money. For most people the decision will be between one of three options:

◆ **repayment** mortgage
◆ **investement backed** mortgage
◆ **pension backed** mortgage.

ASSESSING REPAYMENT MORTGAGES

A repayment mortgage is the simplest type of mortgage. You borrow, say, £50,000 and each year pay back interest on the loan and a little bit of the capital that you borrowed in the first place. Consider the following examples. (Both examples are simplified. In reality the way that annual percentage rates are calculated would mean that the actual payments would be somewhat different.)

Example 1

A £50,000 loan is made over a term of 25 years.

This means that on average each year the capital repayment is £50,000 ÷ 25 years, ie £2,000 per annum.

On top of this interest is payable at say ten per cent.

Thus in the first year the payment is £5,000 interest
£2,000 capital repayment

Repayment £7,000 total

The problem is that a repayment mortgage does not work like this. In order to keep the mortgage payments down in the first years, the mortgage lender reduces the amount of capital that is repaid in the early years of the loan. As the loan decreases, the amount of interest payable each year decreases, and a larger percentage of the repayment becomes available to repay the capital.

Example 2

The same £50,000 loan is made over a 25-year term.

The interest rate is still ten per cent.

The first year's payment is £5,000

£500 capital repayment

Repayment £5,500 total

Whilst this certainly makes the mortgage payments more acceptable, the drawback is that if the borrower moves house again two or three years later they might find that they have repaid very little of the £50,000 that they originally borrowed.

On moving, they would probably take out a new 25-year loan and the whole process would start all over again. If they move house on a regular basis they might still be paying off a mortgage at an age when they wish to retire.

Despite this the great majority of people now opt for a repayment mortgage. However, there are two other alternatives.

ASSESSING INVESTMENT BACKED MORTGAGES

With an investment mortgage, the same £50,000 is borrowed over the same 25-year term. However, the full £50,000 loan remains outstanding for the full 25 years. The average ,2,000 per annum that would have been used to repay the capital is instead invested in an investment policy. This money is used to buy stocks and shares (and is certain cases other investments such as property). The hope is that in 25 years time the value of the investment policy will have increased to a level where it can be used to repay the £50,000 mortgage and possibly provide a surplus for the policy holder to spend as he wishes

Pros and cons of investment mortgages

Investment mortgages and most particularly endowment policies have come in for a lot of criticism in recent years. Much of this is not justified. Endowment policies can and have been an excellent investment for some policy holders. Consider this (true) example.

> An endowment policy was taken out in January 1974 with a top performing insurance company. The sum assured was £50,000 and the term was 25 years. The policy has just matured. The policy holder received just over £160,000. This gave him £50,000 to repay his mortgage and £110,000 to spend as he pleased.

Unfortunately stock market returns have been considerably lower in recent years than they were during the 1970s and 1980s. As a consequence endowment policies taken out during the last ten years have not performed as well as this. Some people who took out a ten-year policy with a poor performing life company, found that their policy did not even provide enough money to repay their mortgage, never mind providing any surplus. These policy holders were faced with the choice between increasing the level of premiums paid into their policy or paying off the shortfall from their own resources.

No one knows how the stock market will perform over the next 25 years. An investment backed mortgage may or may not be a good investment but before you can decide whether it is the best type of mortgage for you, you need to take advice from a suitably qualified professional.

ASSESSING PENSION MORTGAGES

The last option is a pension mortgage. The main advantage of a pension mortgage is that it is very tax efficient. Under current legislation you will receive tax relief on your pension premiums at your highest marginal tax rate.

Assessing the disadvantages

There are at least three disadvantages.

Future eligibility

Pension mortgages can only be funded from a personal pension policy. These are usually taken out by the self-employed or by those whose employer does not provide a company pension scheme. If at some future time you decided to become a member of a company pension scheme, you would have to cease making payments into your personal pension plan and make alternative arrangements to repay your mortgage.

Affordability

A pension mortgage will cost more than an endowment mortgage or a repayment mortgage. The reason for this is that under current legislation only one-quarter of a pension fund can be taken on retirement as a cash lump sum. The remainder must be used to purchase an annuity (this may change in the future). The mortgage can only be repaid from the cash lump sum. Thus in order to fund a pension mortgage of £100,000, you would need to build a pension fund of £400,000.

Income in retirement

Many people feel that the whole of their pension should be used to fund their retirement. By using one-third of your pension fund to repay a mortgage you will significantly reduce you income when you retire.

Investment return

If you do decide to take out an investment backed mortgage or a pension mortgage, it is extremely important to chose a provider with good investment performance. More than 100 life assurance companies compete to offer investment and pension products in the UK market and their performance varies greatly.

Summary

The decision regarding which repayment method is best for you is a complex one. It is essential to take advice from a suitably qualified professional before making a final decision.

CASE STUDY
John pays over the odds

John McD bought a two-bedroomed flat for £30,000 in 1996. He had a County Court Judgement for debt for £1,200 incurred as a result of a dispute over a second-hand car which broke down. He had paid off the debt 18 months before but knew that his CCJ would affect his mortgage application.

John arranged his mortgage through a small mortgage

broker out of the local paper. In view of his CCJ John was thankful to be offered any loan and didn't flinch at the interest rate which was three per cent above the norm.

Three years later John met his future wife and they decided to buy a house together. This time they went to a much larger mortgage broker and again John declared his CCJ. 'That will be no problem at all' said the broker. 'In fact, if you'd come to me three years ago, I could have arranged a loan for you through a major lender. I don't know why you took out the loan that you did.'

John is furious. During those three years he has paid £2,700 more than necessary for his mortgage. Next time he will see more than one broker.

MORTGAGES IN THE FUTURE

There are likely to be two significant changes in the mortgage market in the future.

Greater flexibility

The first is that mortgage lenders will be forced to design more flexible loans. The days when you could expect a job for life have long gone and today's working arrangements are far more varied and flexible. Many people are not employed but work on a contract basis. A lot of people have more than one job. An increasing number of people are becoming self-employed. These changes will require the development of flexible mortgage products that allow borrowers to make higher mortgage payments when they are able to do so and stop making payments entirely when they are between jobs. This is already starting to happen.

A faster process

My second prediction is that the government's attempt to speed up the home buying process will put pressure on lenders to get mortgage offers out more quickly. In practice this is likely to mean that most buyers will choose a mortgage lender, and allow that lender to take employment and financial references before they start looking for a property.

5

Choosing a Property

This chapter will help you make the right compromise between the property that you want and the one that you need.

DECIDING WHAT SORT OF PROPERTY YOU REALLY NEED

We all have a dream house – a penthouse flat, an old rectory, or perhaps a farmhouse set in its own land. While it is nice to dream, unless you have just won the lottery this is not the property that you will actually buy.

For most of us buying a property means making a series of trade-offs and compromises.

The best way to decide on what compromises you are and are not prepared to make is to set your requirements down on paper. Figure 3 shows how the list might look for a family with two young children seeking to buy a three- or four-bedroomed suburban house. Try doing the exercise yourself using the same headings.

EXPLORING THE IMPORTANCE OF LOCATION

The three most important factors in valuing a property are location, location and location.

Need	Want
Bedrooms Minimum three. The children (boy 6, girl 4) are sharing a bedroom now and cannot do so for much longer.	Four – a guest room would be nice, but guests do not stay that often. A sofa bed in one of the living rooms would probably suffice.
Living rooms Two – the only living room in our current property is always strewn with toys and it is driving us mad.	Three – in addition to a playroom, a separate dining room that could also be used as a study would be wonderful, but it would not be used often.
Kitchen Must be large enough to eat in unless there is a separate dining room.	The bigger the better.
Bathrooms One.	With two young children a ground floor toilet would be useful and a second bathroom even better.
Garage Not essential.	Would be nice but it would mostly be used for storage so a garden shed would do.
Garden 60' minimum – the same as we have now.	The bigger the better.
Type of property 1930s semi: a good balance between spacious rooms and reasonable maintenance costs.	Would love a detached property but it's probably out of the price range.
Condition Reasonable order throughout. We are not DIY enthusiasts and using builders is too expensive. Would redecorate but not much more.	In spotless condition throughout.
Location Must be in the catchment area for All Saints Primary School and the James Brown Secondary School.	Would really like to live on the Avenue Gardens estate if we can afford it.
Situation With a dog, a cat and two young children we would not be prepared to live on a main road.	A cul-de-sac would be ideal.
Transport links We would like to be close to the station.	We only use the station two or three days each month so proximity is not essential.

Fig. 3. Example home requirements list.

So says the old estate agents adage and this one is 100 per cent correct. A smaller property in a better area will nearly always be a better buy than a larger property in a poorer one. There are at least four good reasons for this.

Social benefits

Most people are happiest living in an area where there are other people like them. For example, if you have a young family it's nice to know that there are other young families in the area. It would be much harder to feel at home in an inner city area where the majority of your neighbours are students.

Fear of crime

Crime, or more accurately the fear of crime, is another important factor which is encouraging people to head for the relative safety of the established residential areas.

Schooling

Until recently we were led to believe that all schools were the same. The publication of the school league tables has dispelled this myth forever and property within the catchment area of the better schools is increasing in value disproportionately.

Investment

For reasons explained later in this chapter, the value of property in better residential areas has been increasing more quickly than that of property elsewhere. This trend looks set to continue. A smaller property in a better area is therefore likely to be a better investment.

The choice of location will of course involve an element of compromise. A one-bedroomed flat in Mayfair might be an excellent investment but it would hardly be an appropriate place to bring up a family. Nevertheless, when it comes to choosing the location the fewer compromises that you can make the better.

Spotting the up-and-coming areas

The desirability of an area can change very quickly.

Losing value

For example, in one suburb of Manchester property has halved in value during the last five years. The problem started when housing associations bought a few houses and moved some problem tenants in. The existing residents found their new neighbours difficult to live with, and those who could sold their properties and left the area. The sudden increase in the number of properties available led to a drop in prices and this in turn made the area more attractive to the housing associations who bought up more properties. This changed the residential mix of the area permanently and the last of the original residents felt so uncomfortable that they also left. Today the area is almost entirely owned by housing associations and is controlled by problem tenants. It is now such an undesirable place to live that values have plummeted.

Increasing value

The opposite can also occur with equal speed. A good example of an area where prices have increased in the last five years is West Action in west London. West Acton is next to Ealing which has always been a desirable area. Most of the houses are large Victorian and Edwardian properties with four or five bedrooms.

During the 1970s and 80s many of the houses were considered too large for single family occupation and were split up into flats and bedsits. Now the trend is being reversed. Prices in Ealing had risen to such a level that many families could no longer afford to buy there. West Acton was a logical alternative. The properties were very similar to those in Ealing. Transport links were good and the area was within the catchment areas for some good schools.

The trickle of professional families moving into the area became a flood and prices increased sharply. The original residents, mostly young people living in small flats, no longer felt at home and began to move out to more cosmopolitan areas. Today West Acton is almost indistinguishable from Ealing.

Gambling on an area

If you are young, single or married without children and want to gamble on buying a property in an up-and-coming area, you need to look for an area that is adjacent to a good area, has good transport links and access to good schools. If you already have a family, the best advice is to stick to established residential areas.

ASSESSING AN AREA

If you don't know the area that you are intending to buy in, it is well worth spending some time getting to know it properly. First impressions can be very deceptive and ideally you should visit the area at least three times, once on a weekday, once at night and once at a weekend. It is surprising how many apparently quiet streets are plagued by problems such as commuter traffic during the rush hour or gangs of marauding teenagers after dark.

Here are some other useful ways to size up an area.

◆ Visit the local shops – do they sell the sort of things that you buy?
◆ Visit the local pubs – do you feel at home with the locals?
◆ Look at the gardens – are they well maintained and what play equipment is there? This will give you an idea of the ages of the local children.
◆ Count the number of bells on each door – more than one means that the house has been split into flats. This could mean noise and parking problems.
◆ Look (discreetly) through the windows – the curtains, decor and furnishings will give you a good idea of the age and background of the people who live there.
◆ Check out the local transport – try actually doing the journey to work before you commit yourself.
◆ Check out the schools – the league tables are not perfect but they give a good idea of the quality of schooling in the area.

FACTORS THAT MAY REDUCE THE ASKING PRICE

Location is not the same as situation. By compromising over the situation, you might be able to avoid making compromises in other areas. For example, a house on a busy road might sell for 20 or 30 per cent less than an identical house round the corner. Places to look for bargains include:

◆ on a busy road
◆ near a railway line
◆ under a flight path

◆ out of easy reach of shops

◆ outside the catchment area of good schools

◆ next to an industrial or business site

◆ above a shop.

INVESTING IN YOUR HOME

Your home is probably the most expensive thing that you will every buy and you will naturally be anxious to ensure that it turns out to be a good investment. Some research that I did for a *Sunday Times* article confirms the importance of choosing a property in the right location.

We looked at a number of properties bought 15 or 20 years ago and compared their value then to their value today. The results were fascinating. One of the most dramatic results was obtained in Bristol. At one end of the scale we found an example of a two-bedroomed flat in Redland, a prosperous suburb, bought for £8,500 in 1979 and today worth £80,000: an increase of 941 per cent.

At the other end of the scale, we found a three-bedroomed house in Southmead, a less desirable area nearby, valued at £18,000 in 1982 and sold at £18,500 in 1997. An increase of just three per cent over 15 years.

Drawing conclusions

The conclusion of this research was clear. Property in the best residential areas has appreciated in value much more quickly than property elsewhere. On this basis it is worth remembering: whatever you compromise on do not comprise over location, location or location.

CASE STUDIES

Marilyn and Philip ignore location

Marilyn and Philip B had intended to buy a three-bedroomed house in Chiswick but they fell in love with a six-bedroomed house in a less desirable area close by. The house had previously been used as bedsits and required a lot of work, but it had potential and they felt that such a beautiful house would always be easy to resell.

They began to feel unwelcome in the area almost as soon as they moved in. Most of the properties were still arranged as bedsits. They had nothing in common with their neighbours and there were no other children for their girls to play with. The local school was awful. The walk to the station took 15 minutes. A week after they moved in Philip's car was vandalised. The final straw came five months later when they were burgled in broad daylight.

Marilyn and Philip decided to cut their losses and move again. The property proved extremely difficult to sell. It took four months to find a buyer and they did not recover the money that they had spent on refurbishment.

Commenting on her experiences, Marilyn says 'It was such a beautiful house but we just could not put up with the area. We have lost money on the house and had to pay two lots of moving costs. It has been a financial disaster. We are now buying the house in Chiswick that we should have bought in the first place. As a result of our mistake we have a much larger mortgage than we need have had.'

Simon and Katrina find location isn't all

Simon and Katrina J were determined not to compromise over the area. They bought a three-bedroomed semi-detached house in Wilmslow, a very desirable part of Cheshire. The house was smaller than they would have liked but they felt that location was all.

The area was lovely but the house drove them mad. Their two youngest children had to share a bedroom and fought like cat and dog. The dining room became a playroom and the kitchen was not large enough to eat in. The result was that they had to eat most of their meals off their laps. The worst thing, though, was that Katrina, a freelance journalist, had no proper place to work. She had put a desk in the corner of her bedroom but she found it hard to work in the room that she slept in and hard to sleep in the room that she worked in.

After 12 miserable months Simon and Katrina decided to move again, this time to a four-bedroomed Victorian house with three living rooms, in Macclesfield, a pleasant town ten miles away.

Commenting on her experiences, Katrina says 'We took the adage of location, location and location too much to heart and ended up with a house that was too small for our needs. I am cross that we have had the expense and inconvenience of moving twice but there is no doubt in my mind that moving again was the right thing to do.'

(6)

Finding a Property

Once you have decided what type of property you are looking for, this chapter will help you to find it.

GETTING THE BEST OUT OF ESTATE AGENTS

As explained in Chapter 2, estate agents are not on your side.
The estate agent's job is to get the best price for the vendor.
Nevertheless, in order to achieve this, estate agents need to
be nice to purchasers so that they will view the maximum
number of properties. There is a strong correlation between
the number of viewings that are arranged on the property and
the price that is achieved.

For your part you need to make friends with all the estate
agents. By doing so, you will help to ensure that you are told
about all the new properties that come up for sale.

The more properties you see, the better the chance that
you will choose the right one.

How estate agents assess their purchasers

Even in a quiet market, estate agents are contacted by
far more purchasers than they can service effectively.
Most therefore operate a grading system to separate the wheat
from the chaff. A typical grading system would work like
this.

Grade 1 – hot
Definition: Purchaser is able to proceed with a purchase immediately. This means that you:

◆ are a first time buyer
◆ have sold your own property and have a completed chain
◆ are in rented accommodation
◆ are able to proceed without selling your current property.

If you fit into this category you should be told about every new property as soon as it comes onto the market.

Grade 2 – local vendors
Definition: Local vendors cannot proceed immediately because they have their own property yet to sell. If you are a local vendor it means that:

◆ You have a house to sell locally which is not yet on the market.
◆ Your house is already up for sale with another estate agent.
◆ Your house is already up for sale with the same agent that you are trying to buy through.

If you fit into this category you should receive good service from the agents that you contact. However, you should be aware that the agent's prime objective may be to persuade you to instruct them to sell your current property. You are not a hot buyer until you have secured an offer on your own.

Grade 3 – others
Definition: This category covers all purchasers who are moving from out of the area and have a house yet to sell.

If you are not yet in a position to buy, and have no property to sell that the agent can earn a fee on, you will not be a priority for most agents. Some agents will refuse point blank to register you as a buyer until you have got an offer on your own property. Others will register you, but refuse to arrange any viewings until you have sold. This can be extremely frustrating. However, you must see it from the estate agent's point of view. The agent knows that statistically 95 per cent of people who register from out of the area will never buy a property in their town. The only way to ensure that you are taken seriously is to secure an offer on your own property before you start looking seriously

The registration process

It is best to register with the estate agents in person if possible. You will be able to strike up a much better rapport face to face and this will help to ensue that you are the first person that the agent thinks of when a new property comes onto the market. By registering in person you may also get to see details of properties that have only just come onto the market and are not yet ready to be circulated.

The agent will ask you a number of questions and will discreetly grade you as a 'hot buyer', 'potential vendor' or 'other'. If you are a hot buyer or a potential vendor you may be offered the opportunity to view some properties immediately. It is well worth doing so if you have the time. By agreeing to view immediately, you will help to consolidate the agent's impression that you are a serious buyer. Your feedback will also give the agent a more accurate idea about precisely what type of property you are looking for.

Going to all the agents

Do try to make sure that you register with all the agents in the town, even if they don't appear to specialise in the sort of property that you are looking for. The most upmarket agents occasionally deal with bread and butter properties and vice versa. Often such an agent will have relatively few applicants for these properties and this could mean that you pick up a bargain.

Receiving agents' particulars

Once you have registered, the agent should send you particular of all the new properties that come onto the market in your price range. It is likely that you will receive particulars of many properties that do not met even your most basic requirements (a two-bedroomed flat when you wanted a four-bedroomed house). There is no point complaining to the estate agents about this. Many agents deliberately avoid selecting which properties to send in case you are tempted by a long shot.

Since the Property Misdescriptions Act was introduced agents' particulars must by law be accurate. Misdescription of a property is a criminal offence so these days agents' details can be relied upon.

Making telephone contact

Even in a quiet market the best properties come and go very quickly, sometimes before the details have even been prepared. It is therefore essential to ensure that you leave telephone numbers where you can be contacted at any time of day. If you are really anxious to move, it may even be worth telephoning all the agents periodically to see if anything new has come. As the old saying goes, the creaky wheel gets the grease. A telephone call once or twice a week will confirm that you are a serious buyer and will help to ensure that you are at the front of the estate agent's mind when a new property does come onto the market.

Maintaining urgency

The best properties really do sell very quickly, sometimes within hours. If you are offered a chance to view somewhere, it is therefore worth trying to fit in a viewing as soon as possible, even if this means viewing after dark. If the property seems a possibility, you can always return in daylight.

How to behave during a viewing

You would be well advised to say as little as possible when you are viewing a property. If you express enthusiasm for the property, the agent and/or the vendor might take a tougher stance during subsequent negotiations because they believe that you want the property badly.

If on the other you complain loudly about the poky rooms and tired decor, the vendor may be offended and decide that they do not want to sell the property to you at all. The best thing is to keep your thoughts to yourself.

Feeding back

A good agent will call you after every viewing to get your feedback. If the agent doesn't ring, ring them. When giving feedback try to cover the things that you did like as well as those that you didn't, but be honest. Unless you give honest feedback, the agents will not have the information that they need in order to find you the right property.

BUYING PRIVATELY

The great majority of properties are sold through estate agents, but it is possible to buy a property privately. Private sellers are not always aware of the true value of their property and bargains can occasionally be had.

There are three ways to go about finding a property privately.

◆ Private advertisements: Most local papers have a private sellers section at the back.
◆ Advertise yourself: It might be worth trying your own 'wanted' advertisement in the local paper. Describe the property you are seeking, state your price range and make it clear that you are a private buyer and that no commission will be payable.
◆ Leaflet drop: The most successful way to find a property is to leaflet-drop houses in the road that you are interested in. Again, remember to make it clear that you are a private buyer and that no commission will be payable.

USING THE INTERNET

Many house buyers now start their property search on the Internet. There is no doubt that the Internet is becoming more important with each month that goes by.

The majority of estate agents have their own Internet site which allows house buyers to view the properties that that agent has available. In addition most agents subscribe to one of the major property portals. There are several portals but most properties are advertised on only one of them. In order to find all the properties available in an area the Internet buyer will probably have to look on several different sites. The problem is compounded by the fact some of sites are badly out of date and display properties that have been sold several weeks previously.

The Internet is a great place to start but until then the only sure way to find out about all the properties that are for sale in an area is to telephone the estate agents directly.

RETAINING AN AGENT TO ACT FOR YOU

If you do not have the time, the market knowledge or the inclination to look for a property yourself, you could retain an agent to do the job for you. Retained agents, or property search agents as they are often known, tend to specialise in the upper end of the market. If you are looking for this type of property, a good search agent can earn their fee many times over. A good search agent will:

◆ advise you on which areas to consider
◆ advise you on schools, transport and other amenities
◆ help to agree a realistic budget
◆ conduct the first viewing on your behalf
◆ advise on what price to pay
◆ negotiate the purchase on your behalf
◆ help to ensure that the sale goes through smoothly

The fee for this service will typically be one-and-a-half to two per cent of the purchase price plus VAT. Most search agents require a non-refundable deposit before they start work.

COMPILING A SHORT LIST

Once you have viewed a good selection of properties (preferably at least half a dozen) you should be ready to compile a short list. Often the decision is made on the basis of a gut reaction. Some American research found that 50 per cent of all house buyers had made a decision to buy before they got inside the front door and 75 per cent had decided before they left the first room. However, if you are having difficulty deciding between more than one property, it may be useful to compare each against your original criteria (see Chapter 5).

CHECKING OUT THE CHAIN

One very important last factor to consider is the owners. Do you trust them? How well does their timescale match yours? If you need to be in within four weeks and their new home will not be ready for three months, you may need to find somewhere else.

One final factor to consider is the length of the chain. Your vendors might be the nicest people in the world but they will not be able to move if they are let down by someone higher up the chain. Before you decide whether to make an offer ask the estate agent for as much information as possible about the upward chain. The more people there are in it the more likely it is that something will go wrong.

Many years experience has taught me to be particularly suspicious about people who are divorcing. The problem is that if they are buying separate properties the number of people incolved in the upward chain and therefore the chance of something going wrong can increase significantly.

BUYING A HOME IN THE FUTURE

The home seller's pack that the Government is proposing to introduce (see Chapter 2) should mean that far more information is available to you before you make an offer.

It is my belief that market forces may lead to the introduction of many of these practices in advance of the legislation. By the time you are reading this, vendor surveys and the advance provision of searches, pre-contract enquiries and leases may have already become common practice.

If this is the case, it is important not to be rushed into making an offer before you have had time to digest all the available information.

It is always more difficult to reduce an over-generous offer after it has been made than to persuade the vendor to accept a fair offer in the first place.

CASE STUDY
Julie's and Patrick's persistence pays off

Julie and Patrick M were in a tearing hurry to buy a property. They had moved to Bath from London and were renting a flat from Patrick's employer. They very much wanted a home of their own. They registered with every agent in the area in person and Julie telephoned them all twice a week. Their persistence paid off when a delightful three-bedroomed cottage came onto the market. The agent telephoned Julie at 9.30 am, both she and Patrick viewed at 1.30 pm and they made an offer at 2.30 pm. The offer was accepted the following morning and they moved in six weeks later.

Commenting on her home buying experience, Julie says 'I probably made a bit of a nuisance of myself but it paid off in the end. We are delighted with our new home.'

$$\boxed{7}$$

Negotiating the
Purchase Price

This chapter will help you to make sure that you pay a fair price for your chosen property.

HOW TO ASSESS THE VALUE OF A PROPERTY
Using the comparables method

Estate agents value properties by comparing them with similar properties in the area. These properties fall into two categories:

◆ properties that are currently for sale in the same price range and are therefore competing for the same buyers
◆ and properties that have recently been sold where the actual price achieved is known.

You need to make your assessment of the value of the property that you are intending to buy using the same method.

Before you make your offer try to obtain as many details of other properties in the area as possible. Properties that are still available will be listed on the estate agents' web sites and on the major property portals. Details of the actual selling prices achieved for similar properties that have sold in the area can be obtained from the Land Registry web site (www.landregisteronline.gov.uk) or from a variety of other web-based information providers.

How do the properties that you have found compare? If you are buying an estate-type property you may be able to find comparables that are almost identical to the one that you are considering. Valuing this type of property is relatively easy.

Using adjustment factors

If you are intending to buy a more individual property, you will need to apply a number of adjustment factors to the comparable properties that are available. Some of the most important factors to take into account are listed below.

Extensions and improvements
The full cost of extensions and improvements will not generally be recovered. The proportion of the original cost that is recovered will depend upon the nature of the improvement, as below.

High cost-recovery (up to 100 per cent):

◆ addition of extra bedroom in a style that is in keeping with the original property
◆ redecoration in a neutral style.

Medium cost-recovery (up to 50 per cent):

◆ addition of ground floor flat-roofed extension
◆ fitted kitchen
◆ loft conversion.

Low cost-recovery (less than 25 per cent):

◆ addition of outdoor swimming pool
◆ double glazing.

Some improvements can substantially *reduce* the value of the property, for example:

◆ extensions that occupy the entire garden
◆ ugly double glazing on period property.

Repairs
As with improvements, the full cost of repairs made to the property is unlikely to be recovered. Many buyers underestimate the cost of repairs and some are prepared to pay a premium for a house in poor condition in order to have the satisfaction of refurbishing it in their own taste.

Area
In many towns a house in one road can command a very substantial premium over houses in the next. It is impossible to generalise about this but the boundaries are usually well known locally.

Location
A house on a busy road, or one backing onto a railway line, will be worth substantially less than an identical house in a quiet street nearby. An extremely adverse location could reduce the value of a property by up to half.

New developments
Many people will pay a premium to live in a brand-new

house. All new developments must therefore be excluded from your comparable evidence.

Square footage/meterage method
A method of valuation that is used extensively abroad but quite seldom in the UK is square footage. If you are having difficulty coming up with a value for an unusual property, it may be worth calculating the price per square foot. Divide the asking price by the total floor area. For example:

Asking price: £100,000
Floor area: 1000 sq.ft.
Price per sq.ft. £100

Then try doing the same calculation for similar properties that are for sale in the same price range.

Asking the vendor

One final option is to ask the vendor or the estate agent to justify the price that is being asked. Say that you are thinking of making an offer and the price looks a little steep and ask them how they arrived at their figure. What supporting evidence are they able to provide? Do their arguments seem convincing?

MAKING AN OFFER

It is best to make the initial offer in writing if possible. This will help to ensure that your offer is communicated accurately and will help to avoid future misunderstandings or disputes about who said what. In the interest of speed a fax is best.

The initial letter should:

◆ be clearly marked 'Subject to Contract'
◆ summarise the benefits of your buying position and your timescale
◆ state the price offered
◆ justify the price offered
◆ list any other conditions.

See the example in Figure 4.

CASE STUDY
Sharon offers too little

Sharon W viewed a flat that was on the market at £49,950. During the viewing the vendor made the mistake of telling Sharon that they had just had an offer accepted on a house that they really loved. Knowing that the vendor was in a hurry to move Sharon decided to try a cheeky offer of £40,000. The vendor rejected it out of hand and said that the offer was so insulting that he would not now consider selling Sharon the flat at any price. Three days later the flat was sold to someone else for £48,000.

Commenting on her experience, Sharon says, 'I liked the flat and it was worth £49,950. With hindsight I wish that I had gone in with a more reasonable opening offer.'

Dear Mr Jones,

Re: 27 Avenue Gardens, Anytown
SUBJECT TO CONTRACT

I should like to make an offer to purchase your property.

I am in an excellent position to proceed quickly. I am in rented accommodation at the moment and I have no property to sell. I have a large deposit and my mortgage is already arranged. I could probably exchange contracts within four to six weeks.

I should like to make an offer of £65,000. I feel that this is a fair price for the property because a sale was agreed at this figure on 17 Avenue Gardens three weeks ago. Number 34 is also up for sale at £65,950.

My offer is subject to survey and subject to you taking the property off the market immediately.

I hope that my offer is acceptable to you and I look forward to hearing from you shortly.

Yours sincerely

P Smith

Fig. 4. Making an offer.

HANDLING THE NEGOTIATIONS

The traditional process of negotiation is highly confrontational. The parties start off a few thousand pounds apart and each side takes turns to increase or decrease the price that they are prepared to pay or accept.

The problem is that each concession makes the parties more determined not to give in again and all too often the negotiations reach deadlock. Sometimes the issue left unresolved is trivial to the point of farce. Most estate agents can tell a story about a sale that did not proceed because of a dispute over a garden shed, a tired old stair carpet or even a wooden toilet seat.

Dear Mr Smith

Re: 27 Avenue Gardens, Anytown
SUBJECT TO CONTRACT

Thank you for your offer to buy our property. I am afraid that we cannot afford to take less than £69,000.

Yours sincerely

Mr Jones

Dear Mr Jones

Re: 27 Avenue Gardens, Anytown
SUBJECT TO CONTRACT

I am sorry to hear that you cannot accept our offer. Before I consider increasing it, could you tell me how you arrived at your valuation of £69,000.
I look forward to hearing from you.

Yours sincerely

P Smith

Dear Mr Smith

Re:27 Avenue Gardens, Anytown
SUBJECT TO CONTRACT

17 Avenue Gardens was in poor condition and required redecoration. No. 34 has no garage. I feel therefore that our property is worth £69,000.

Yours sincerely

Mr Jones

Fig. 5. Negotiating the price.

Dear Mr Jones

Re:27 Avenue Gardens, Anytown
SUBJECT TO CONTRACT

I agree that No. 17 was in poor condition and on this basis I am prepared to raise my offer to £67,000. I feel that this is a fair offer and I hope that you will now accept it. May I remind you again that we can move very quickly.

Yours sincerely

P Smith

Dear Mr Smith

Re:27 Avenue Gardens, Anytown
SUBJECT TO CONTRACT

Thank you for your revised offer which I am prepared to accept provided that you exchange contracts within six weeks. Please contact my estate agent to arrange all the final details.

Yours sincerely

Mr Jones

Fig. 5. Cont.

Asking for justification

The way to avoid this is to keep asking the simple questions 'why' and 'how'. If the vendor rejects your first offer, ask them why they have rejected it and how they have arrived at the figure they require. The correspondence might continue as in Figure 5. The technique of asking the other party to justify their position works like a magic charm and can be used several times during the same negotiation.

COMPETING WITH OTHER WOULD-BE PURCHASERS

Even in a quiet market, the vendors of the best properties often receive more than one offer. The way to get your offer accepted is to sell the benefits of your buying position to the vendor. For example, if you know that the vendor needs to move quickly, stress the speed with which you can move.

By finding out what the vendor is hoping to achieve and making your buying position match these needs, you will often be able to get your offer accepted without increasing the price.

Sealed bids

When a property is in great demand, the agent will sometimes advise going to sealed bids. Would-be purchasers are asked to make their best and final offer in writing by a given date. The difficulty when deciding what offer to make is that you do not know what other parties have offered. If you are determined to secure the property a good way to do so is to bid an odd amount, e.g. £111,111. Most people bid in round figures so you might win the contest by £1.

When making a sealed bid remember to include details of your buying position. The vendor is not obliged to accept the highest bid, and if you are in a strong position she may decide to accept your offer even if she has a higher one.

KNOWING WHEN TO WALK AWAY

It is all too easy to get caught up in a bidding fever. A house on the River Thames at Henley once sold for twice its asking price because two people were absolutely determined to have it. You may be able to justify paying a little over the odds to secure a house that you love, but there comes a point when it is better to wait for the next one to come along.

Another thing to bear in mind is that if you agree to pay significantly over the odds, the property could be down-valued by the building society surveyor. This may prevent you from proceeding with the purchase anyway.

CASE STUDY
Sanjay knows when to walk away

Sanjay P made an offer to pay £110,000 for a house that was on the market at £130,000. He had researched the offer carefully and felt that his offer was a fair one. The vendor rejected it out of hand and said that he wanted the asking price.

Sanjay asked the vendor to justify his figure of £130,000. The vendor said that this was the price that he needed in order to buy his next property. Sanjay pointed out that this was no reason for him to pay over the odds and cited two comparable properties that had sold recently for £110,000 and £112,000 respectively. The vendor would not budge and Sanjay walked away.

Three weeks later Sanjay had an offer accepted to buy a virtually identical property in the next street at £112,500. The property that he walked away from remains unsold.

(8)

Choosing A Solicitor

A good solicitor will make your purchase quicker, less stressful and much less likely to fall through. This chapter will help you to make the right choice.

THE IMPORTANCE OF CHOOSING THE RIGHT SOLICITOR

There are two key dangers that you need to guard against. The first is a solicitor who is slow, inefficient, or unnecessarily pedantic. A consequence of instructing such a solicitor could be that you lose the property that you were trying to buy.

An even worse danger is posed by the solicitor who is overworked, inexperienced in conveyancing matters or does not check the documentation carefully enough. If you instruct a solicitor like this, you could end up buying a property that later proves to be impossible to resell.

KNOWING HOW TO CHOOSE A SOLICITOR
Choosing a specialist

If you had a brain tumour you would seek the advice of a brain surgeon. You would not expect your family doctor to perform the operation on you himself and you would certainly not seek advice from a gynaecologist just because she happened to be a family friend.

For exactly the same reasons, if you are buying a property

you should not automatically go to your local family solicitor and you should almost certainly avoid using the solicitor who you met whilst he was advising your employer on tax. Conveyancing is a specialist area of the law and you need a conveyancing specialist, not a general practitioner or a tax specialist.

Before you instruct a solicitor to handle your conveyancing work, check to make sure that the firm specialises in residential conveyancing.

This means that it has at least one person in the firm who deals with conveyancing all the time. Such firms will have come across all the common problems before, and will have the systems and knowledge necessary to have the best chance of resolving any problems that may come up with your purchase.

Asking for recommendations

One of the best ways to choose a solicitor is by recommendation. If you know someone who has bought a house recently, ask which solicitor they used and what they thought of them. It is also worth asking your estate agent and/or mortgage broker for a recommendation. They deal with solicitors on a daily basis and will have a very good idea of which local firms are most efficient.

Never choosing on price alone

Fees for conveyancing work vary enormously, but a conveyancing solicitor should never be chosen on price alone. If a solicitor gives a quote that is significantly cheaper than his competitors it will usually mean one of two things.

◆ Most of the work will be handled by an unqualified (and therefore cheaper) legal assistant.
◆ The solicitor has budgeted to spend less time on your case.

The consequences of this could be:

◆ Documents might be examined less thoroughly.
◆ It might be hard to get hold of your solicitor if you have any questions or if a problem needs to be resolved.
◆ The sale might take longer than necessary to go through.
◆ The chances of making a mistake are increased.

The adage 'you get what you pay for' holds true in most areas of life and certainly applies when choosing a conveyancing solicitor.

Getting more than one quote

These days most solicitors are very pleased to give you a quote over the telephone. Try to ring at least three firms if possible. The brief conversation that you have with each will help to ensure that you pick someone with whom you feel comfortable as well as comparing fees.

Choosing early

It is best to choose a solicitor before you start looking seriously for a property. If you are selling a property as well as buying, your solicitor will be able to start work on obtaining the title deeds and preparing a draft contract. This will save time once you find a buyer.

Even if you are buying for the first time, it is best to find a solicitor before you find somewhere. Choosing a solicitor is such an important decision that it is best to avoid having to do it in a hurry.

ASKING QUESTIONS BEFORE INSTRUCTING A SOLICITOR

Ask to speak to a partner in the conveyancing department. Say that you are buying a property and want a quote for conveyancing. The solicitor will probably start by asking you some questions about the property so that she or he can give you an accurate quote.

Here are some questions to ask once they have finished:

◆ What does the quote include?
◆ What does the quote exclude?
◆ Does the firm specialise in residential conveyancing?
◆ Roughly how many conveyancing cases does the firm deal with in a typical year?
◆ Ask if the firm is on the 'panel' for the mortgage lender which you are intending to use (if they are not, the mortgage lender will probably want to instruct another solicitor to protect their interest, which will cause unnecessary delay and add to the cost).
◆ Who will actually handle the work?
◆ Why should I instruct your firm to handle my conveyancing rather than the other firms that I have spoken to?

THE ALTERNATIVES TO INSTRUCTING A SOLICITOR

The great majority of house buyers (about 70 per cent) still use a local conveyancing solicitor. However, a conveyancing market is changing quite quickly and there are now a number of alternatives.

Licensed conveyancers

The Society of Licensed Conveyancers was set up to break the solicitor's monopoly of the conveyancing market. In practice they have captured only a small share of it. Most licensed conveyancers work for small local firms and offer a service that is quite similar to that offered by solicitors. Like solicitors many compete on price rather than on service.

Solicitors marketing agencies

The first solicitors marketing agency was set up in 1993. Several now operate in the UK market. The marketing agency obtains conveyancing work both by approaching estate agents and by advertising its service directly to the public. The actual conveyancing work is passed on to independent firms of conveyancing solicitors who are appointed on a panel basis. The solicitors marketing agency charges a mark-up on the cost of the solicitor's work. In return, they employ a customer care team whose job it is to keep the customer informed of all progress on their sale or purchase.

The main benefit of dealing with a solicitors marketing agency is that they are open very long hours and offer high levels of customer service. The drawback is the additional cost.

Estate agent owned conveyancing operations

Countrywide, the UK's largest firm of estate agents, set up its own conveyancing division, in 1997. Countrywide took the solicitors marketing agency concept one stage further by employing its own team of licensed conveyancers rather than passing out the work to outside firms. It seems likely that other estate agency firms will soon start to offer a similar service.

This type of operation offers several important benefits, including convenience, long opening hours and generally high standards of customer care. They can also speed up average transaction times. Countrywide has agreed detailed protocols (eg semi-standardised pre-contract enquiries) with three independent firms of solicitors. In cases where one party is using Countrywide Conveyancing and the other party is using one of these three recommended firms, average transaction times have been reduced quite considerably. The main drawback again is cost.

National conveyancing solicitors

Several major firms of solicitors have opened their own express conveyancing operations to compete with the estate agents and the solicitor marketing agencies. They offer long opening hours, enhanced service levels and a dedicated customer care team to keep clients informed of all progress. Despite the premium fee levels I would predict that this type of operation, which competes on service rather than price alone, will quickly take a significant share of the conveyancing market.

Doing your own conveyancing

It is perfectly possible to do your own conveyancing. Provided that you are buying a freehold property with registered title, the procedures are quite straightforward. DIY conveyancing guides are available to help you complete all the necessary stages correctly.

However, in practice very few people handle their own conveyancing. There are three reasons for this

1. The first is that where a mortgage is involved, the mortgage lender will insist on employing a solicitor to protect its interests. You will be expected to pay for this. This reduces the potential saving on legal fees considerably.

2. The second reason is that the consequences of missing something can be appalling. At worst you could end up buying a property that proves to be impossible to resell.

3. The third problem is that other people involved in the transaction may take a dim view of you handling your own conveyancing. The estate agent may advise the vendor not to accept your offer for fear that your inexperience of conveyancing matters might delay the sale. The solicitor acting for the other side might also be deliberately pedantic in order to try to trip you up.

Taking everything into account there are very few circumstances where it is advisable for you to handle your own conveyancing.

HOW NEW LEGISLATION MAY AFFECT THE PROCESS

The proposal to make a Home Information Pack compulsory is likely to speed up the conveyancing process considerably.

If you are selling as well as buying, you will probably, in the future, have to instruct a solicitor to help you to prepare the information pack before you can put your own property onto the market. If you are buying for the first time it will become even more important in the future to choose a solicitor before you start looking seriously.

A second consequence of speeding up the conveyancing process is likely to be that large companies which offer a premium service at a premium fee, are likely to increase their share of the conveyancing market at the expense of the traditional High Street solicitors.

CASE STUDY
Colin's cheap solicitor proves expensive

Colin A bought his first home in 1988. The property was a two-bedroomed first floor flat which had been newly converted from a Victorian two-storey house. Colin rang round for conveyancing quotes and took the cheapest one. The solicitor that he chose was not terribly helpful. It was extremely hard to get hold of him, and when he did answer the phone he sounded harassed and eager to end the call. On several occasions he failed to return Colin's calls. Nevertheless the purchase eventually went through.

Four years later Colin's employers offered him a better job in Newcastle. Colin decided to sell the property. A sale was agreed very quickly. This time Colin used a different solicitor.

Two weeks into the sale Colin received a phone call from his estate agent. The agent said that the buyer had pulled out due to a defect in the lease. Colin rang his solicitor for an explanation. To his horror he learned that the lease should have given him the right to walk across the front garden, which was owned by the ground floor flat, in order to reach his front door. Unfortunately the developer who sold him the flat had forgotten to put this clause in the lease and his original solicitor had failed to notice. According to the terms of the lease Colin had no right to use his own front path in order to reach his own front door.

Before he could sell the flat, Colin had to apply to his freeholder for a 'Deed of Variation', ie permission to change the defective clause in the lease. His freeholder demanded payment of £1,000 for his 'inconvenience' plus legal costs. The total was nearly £1,500. On top of this Colin's sale was delayed by six months. As a result his employer withdrew the job offer in Newcastle.

Commenting on his experience, Colin says 'My original solicitor was clearly negligent. As a result I have been left £1,500 out of pocket and my promotion at work has been delayed. I shall be pursuing a claim for damages against my original solicitor, but I've no idea how long it will take or whether I will eventually be successful. I have learnt the hard way about the importance of choosing a solicitor with care.'

Choosing a Surveyor

This chapter will help you to decide what type of survey you need and give advice on how to choose the right surveyor.

CONSIDERING IF YOU REALLY NEED A SURVEYOR
Buying for cash

If you are buying a property for cash, you could buy without a survey. However, you would be most unwise to do so. The vast majority of cash buyers do instruct a surveyor to check the property over before they exchange contracts.

CASE STUDY
James and Oonagh find hidden defects

James McL and his wife Oonagh bought a four-bedroomed Victorian property near Leeds for £250,000 with a £100,000 mortgage. They relied entirely on the mortgage valuation and did not instruct a surveyor of their own. On moving into the property James and Oonagh found that it was riddled with problems. There was damp in their daughter's bedroom caused by a leaking roof. There was damp in the kitchen caused by a defective damp course. The wiring was lethal and seemed to blow a fuse most days. The heating and plumbing seemed to have been installed by someone who was drunk and blind as well as incompetent. In total James and Oonagh spent £25,000 putting things right.

James rang his mortgage lender and complained that the surveyor who had carried out the mortgage valuation was incompetent. The lender explained that the surveyor's job was only to confirm that the property was satisfactory security for the £100,000 advance which was secured upon it. The surveyor had no duty of care to James and Oonagh.

Commenting on his experience, James says, 'I assumed that the building society surveyor would survey the property. I had no idea that his inspection would be so cursory. I really feel that the lender should have advised me to instruct my own surveyor. I shall certainly do so next time.'

Buying with a mortgage

The confusion sets in when a mortgage is involved. If you are buying a property on a mortgage, the lender will insist that a surveyor visits the property to undertake a valuation for mortgage purposes. Many people assume that this is all the protection that they need.

Approximately 80 per cent of all home buyers do not instruct their own surveyor and rely entirely upon the building society's report and valuation. They are wrong to do so.

The purpose of a building society report and valuation is to confirm to the mortgage lender that the property which you are buying is satisfactory security for the mortgage advance that is to be secured upon it. Thus if you are buying a property for £100,000, and are applying for a £30,000 mortgage, the surveyor's job is to confirm that the property is worth at least £30,000. Of course it is. If the house fell down tomorrow the site would be worth £30,000. Before you buy the property you need to know rather more than this, specifically:

◆ Is the property worth the price that you are paying for it?
◆ Are there any serious structural defects that might affect your decision to proceed with the purchase?
◆ Are there any less serious defects and if so approximately how much will they cost to rectify?

The only way to establish this information, will be to instruct your own surveyor.

CHOOSING THE TYPE OF SURVEY YOU NEED
Home buyers report
The RICS/ISVA **Home Buyers Report** is prepared in a standard format in order to keep costs down. The main objective of the home buyers report is to:

◆ Reassure you that you are paying a fair price for the property.
◆ Inform you about any serious defects that may affect your decision to proceed with the purchase.

◆ Inform you about any less serious defects which may affect the price that you are prepared to pay for the property.

A home buyers report is likely to be the most appropriate choice if the property that you are buying is:

◆ built after 1919

◆ of a traditional construction

◆ free from obvious structural defects.

In 1999 the typical cost of a home buyers report for an average sized property was around £250 plus VAT. In addition to buyingpeace of mind, many buyers find that they are able to recoup the cost of their survey by using it as a negotiating tool in subsequent price negotiations.

Building survey

A **building survey** is more comprehensive than a home buyers report and is not prepared in a standard format. A building survey may be the best choice if:

◆ The property you are buying was built before 1919.

◆ The property is of a non-standard construction (eg it has a thatched roof or stone walls).

◆ The property is in poor condition and/or has an obvious structural defect (eg a crack in the wall, or a wonky door or window frame).

◆ The property is particularly large or expensive.

The typical cost of a building survey on an average sized property in 2005 was around £500 plus VAT. The cost of a building survey on a very large or unusual property could be several times as much.

Structural engineer's report

If the surveyor suspects that the property may have a structural defect he may advise you to commission a specialist **structural engineer's report**. A structural engineer will assess whether the defect presents a risk to the future stability of the building and advise on what action needs to be taken in order to rectify the problem.

From a safety point of view, surveyors and structural engineers tend to err heavily on the side of caution. Much of the repair work that they advise is unnecessary. However, from a resale point of view any property with a structural defect may prove extremely difficult to sell; unless the property that you are considering is exceptionally good value you should think very carefully before proceeding.

The cost of a structural engineer's report will vary considerably according to the nature of the fault that they are investigating. Ask for a quote before you proceed.

Quantity surveyor's report

If the property that you are buying requires very extensive works, it may be worth instructing a quantity surveyor to prepare a detailed 'bill of works'. This is a detailed estimate of the likely costs. A bill of works may help you to renegotiate the purchase price. It will also help you later on when it comes to getting building estimates and supervising the work.

Timber report

It is quite common for a surveyor to ask for a timber report. If there is evidence of woodworm, wet rot or dry rot a specialist company will be called in to assess the extent of the problem and the cost of rectifying it.

Bear in mind that most timber companies provide reports free of charge and are paid only if they are employed to deal with the problem. It is therefore in their interest to find work that needs doing. The problems that they find are likely to fall into three categories.

Woodworm
Many older houses have had an attack of woodworm at some time in the past. Woodworm is easy to spot. The affected wood has lots of tiny holes almost as if somebody has been throwing darts at it. It can affect any internal or external timber, for example floorboards, windows, doors etc. Unless the owner is able to provide a written guarantee that the problem has been treated it is highly probable that you will have to treat the wood again. Fortunately woodworm is relatively cheap to treat.

Wet rot
Wet rot is caused by the prolonged exposure of untreated timber to rainwater or severe damp. It can affect any external timber or internal timber that has become exceptionally damp. Timber that has not been regularly painted is particularly susceptible.

Wet rot is fairly easy to spot, the timber feels damp and spongy to the touch. It may be treated either by a local builder or by a specialist timber treatment company.

Dry rot

Dry rot is caused by a fungus called *serpula lacrynens*. It is by far the most serious of the three problems and the most expensive one to treat. Dry rot is caused when a damp void such as a cellar, the space beneath the floorboards or a chimney breast is left without sufficient ventilation.

Dry rot is easy to recognise. Affected timbers have distinctive cracks which go along and across the grain causing tiny oblong shapes. The fungus itself looks like a flat white pancake. There is also often a heavy, musty smell. The problem is that the attack often starts beneath a floor or inside a chimney breast and is not discovered until it has caused extensive damage.

Treatment involves replacement of all the affected timber. In order to ensure that the attack does not reoccur it is also necessary to strip off the plaster and pull up floors in adjacent areas so that the timber can be treated with a chemical preventative. If anything is missed, the dry rot will recur.

The cost of treating a dry rot can run into many thousands of pounds. If the property that you are buying has dry rot the safest thing to do is to run a mile. If you do not, be sure to get detailed estimates before proceeding.

Damp reports

It is also common for the surveyor to ask for a damp report. If the moisture content of the walls seems unusually high, the surveyor will recommend that a specialist damp company should be called in to identify the cause of the problem and estimate for the cost of rectifying it.

Like timber companies, most damp companies undertake surveys free of charge and are paid only if they find work that needs doing. This means that they have a vested interest in finding work that needs to be done. The problems that you are most likely to find come into three categories.

Rising damp

Rising damp is caused when the damp course breaks down and the bricks in the walls, which are porous, start to suck up water from the ground. In time, the dampness rises to a level approximately one metre above the ground.

Severe cases are easy to spot. Wallpaper becomes discoloured and starts to peel off the walls. Paint becomes discoloured and often starts to blister. Some home owners try to disguise the problem by putting on lots of layers of wallpaper or even panelling the lower half of the walls. Treatment involves injecting a chemical into the base of the wall to stop the dampness and replacing the plaster up to a height of about one metre.

The problem is that this treatment is often recommended when moisture levels are much lower. In such cases it is often best to just live with the problem. A second problem is that the cause of dampness might be something altogether different (see later) and the treatment proposed quite unnecessary. The best advice is:

 Check for other sources of dampness before proceeding.

◆ If the problem is not serious try living with it for a bit before acting.

◆ Get more than one estimate before proceeding.

Penetrative damp

This type of dampness is caused by a leaking roof, gutter, window frame or something similar. It will normally be rectified by a local builder rather than by a damp treatment company. The treatment is to find and rectify the cause of the leak, then to replace the affected plaster.

Damp caused by incorrect ground levels

A very common cause of dampness is incorrect ground levels. If the level of the ground outside is above the level of the damp course, dampness will be sucked up from the ground. Before proceeding with any damp treatment go outside and look for the damp course. In most buildings this will run horizontally around the building about six inches or so above the ground. Look for a line of bitumen or slate between two courses of bricks. If the ground level is higher than the damp course in any area it will need to be reduced.

CASE STUDY
An extra survey repays Anne and Hamish

Anne G and her husband Hamish bought a large house in rural Devon for £250,000. In addition to the mortgage valuation, they commissioned a full building survey which revealed a number of expensive problems. The roof had been re-covered with the wrong tiles. The new ones were too heavy. They had caused serious structural damage and would have to be replaced. The electrical system was in urgent need of renewal. Worst of all the septic tank in the garden was leaking. The total cost of the repairs came to nearly £30,000.

Anne and Hamish showed the report to the seller and asked for a reduction of £30,000 from the asking price. The owner accepted that the repairs were necessary and after a couple of rounds of negotiation a revised price of £225,000 was agreed.

Commenting on her experiences, Anne says, 'Our survey seemed expensive at the time but it paid for itself many times over. It really proved to be an excellent investment.'

BUYING A BRAND NEW PROPERTY

The great majority of new properties are protected by an NHBC warranty. If the property that you are considering does not have an NHBC certificate, you should proceed only with the greatest ofcaution. It will be essential to commission your own survey in order to check that the property has been built to a satisfactory standard. Even if the survey does give the property a clean bill of health, you need to bear in mind that a new property which does not have an NHBC certificate might be quite difficult to resell.

Knowing what the warranty covers

If the property that you are buying does have a NHBC warranty it will be guaranteed for ten years against structural defects. There is therefore probably no need to commission your own structural survey. However, it is important to appreciate that the NHBC warranty only covers major defects. It does not cover the cost of rectifying the more minor teething problems that seem to affect so many new homes.

There are five things you can do to reduce the chance of buying a defective new home:

◆ Buy from a developer with a reputation for quality. The new homes industry runs its own awards scheme.

◆ Don't just view the show home. Ask to inspect several other properties on the site before you buy and make your own assessment of the quality of the finish.

◆ Try to talk to other people on the site and ask if they have experienced any teething problems with their properties. If so, how efficiently did the developer deal with them?

◆ Telephone the after-sales office on some pretext or visit it if it is on-site. These are the people who will be responsible for rectifying any defects. Their attitude speaks volumes about the developer's attitude to customer service.

◆ Consider visiting other developments built by the same developer in the area. Do they still look bright and new? Again try to talk to some of the residents and see if they have had any problems.

CHOOSING A SURVEYOR

Surveyors are not all the same and it is well worth taking some time to find a good one. Ask your solicitor, your mortgage lender, your estate agents and any friends who have bought a property recently for recommendations. Ring several firms before you make a final decision. Here are some questions that you can ask:

◆ Are you on the panel for the mortgage lender that I am using? This is very important. If the surveyor is on the panel (ie approved by) your mortgage lender he or she will be able to carry out the home buyers report or building survey at the same time as the mortgage valuation. This will save both time and money.

◆ Where are you based? A local surveyor will know about any specific problems that affect the local housing stock and is also likely to have a better idea of local values than someone who is based many miles away.

◆ How quickly could you get me the report? Every day's delay is another day when something could go wrong.

◆ Can I telephone you to discuss the report? This is also very important. If any aspect of the report is unclear, you must be able to clarify it.

◆ Why should I instruct your firm to carry out my survey? A good answer would include issues such as experience, local knowledge and quick turn around times.

◆ How much will it cost? Fees vary significantly from firm to firm. However, the final decision should not be based on price alone.

GETTING THE BEST OUT OF YOUR SURVEYOR

There are two things that you should do to ensure that you get full value out of your survey report.

The first is to let the surveyor know about any specific

concerns that you have about the property (eg a crack in the wall or a wonky door frame). This must be done before their visit and will ensure that you get the necessary reassurance or otherwise.

The second thing is to send the surveyor particulars of any other properties that are for sale or recently sold in the area. The more comparables a surveyor has available, the more accurate will be the valuation. This is particularly important if you are using a surveyor from out of the area.

CASE STUDY
Samantha regrets using a non-local surveyor

Samantha B agreed to buy a two-bedroomed maisonette near Romford, Essex, for £65,000. She instructed her mortgage lender to undertake a combined mortgage valuation and home buyers reports, and used the surveyor they recommended who was based 35 miles away.

To her great disappointment the property was down-valued on survey to £62,000. She asked the vendor to reduce the sale price but he would not budge. She withdrew from the purchase and started to look at alternative properties.

A week later she had not found anything nearly as nice as the original flat, so she rang the agent to say that she would like to proceed with the purchase after all. Too late, the agent said. Another buyer, at £66,000 this time, had already been found. Samantha eventually bought an identical property further down the road. She paid £66,500 for it.

Commenting on her experience, Samantha says, 'With hindsight it is clear that the surveyor's valuation of £62,000 was wrong. It was simply not possible to buy a flat in that road for that price. The second time I instructed a local surveyor and had no problems with the valuation. But I ended up paying £1,500 more than I need have done. I am cross about the whole thing. I should have relied on my own instincts and proceeded with the original purchase.'

INTERPRETING THE REPORT

The surveyor's job is to point out every defect with the property. If he or she does not, they might be sued for negligence. Consequently a survey report can make even a nice property sound in quite poor condition. Generally speaking the surveyor's comments can be divided into one of three categories.

Urgent matters

These are defects that are judged to be an actual or developing threat to the fabric of the building or to personal safety. Such defects will have to be rectified immediately and may affect your decision to proceed with the purchase.

Significant matters

These are defects that you would not necessarily see for yourself and which might affect the price that you are prepared to pay for the property.

Observations

These are things that you could reasonably have been expected to see for yourself, eg the kitchen is old-fashioned or the window frames need redecorating. The surveyor has to include such observations in the report but you are unlikely to be able to use the existence of such defects to renegotiate the price.

If you are in any doubt about the seriousness of any defect you should phone the surveyor and ask for clarification. Most will be pleased to hear from you and may well be a lot more forthcoming off the record than they were in writing.

CASE STUDY
Mary gets a second opinion

Mary P bought a two-bedroomed garden flat in Hampstead, North London. She commissioned a home buyers report which showed that the property was damp along the whole of the front wall.

The surveyor advised a specialist damp report. The damp report said that the damp course was defective and needed replacing. The plaster in both front rooms and the hallway would also need to be replaced. The total estimate was £4,000.

Mary decided to proceed with her purchase regardless. However, before undertaking the work she asked a local builder to give her a second opinion on the dampness.

His conclusion was very different. He pointed out that the gravel drive was above the level of the damp course in several places. He felt that this was the likely cause of the damp.

Two days with a shovel and the problem was cured. By the summer the wall had dried out entirely. Mary covered up the discoloured plaster with some thick wallpaper and a proprietary sealant and spent the £3,500 that she had saved on a new car.

INTERPRETING THE VALUATION

Surveyors' valuations tend to err on the side of caution. It is not uncommon to find that the valuation for mortgage purposes is less than the purchase price that has been agreed.

However, if the difference is more than about five per cent, it could be that the price you have agreed to pay is too high. In such cases the best thing to do is to telephone the surveyor and ask how the valuation has been reached. If they persuade you that you have agreed to pay too much it may be necessary to renegotiate the purchase price (see later).

HOW NEW LEGISLATION MAY AFFECT THE PROCESS

It seems likely that from 2007 sellers will be required to provide a "condition report" on their property as part of the Home Information Pack. This is by far the most contentious aspect of the new legislation. The condition report will not include a valuation of the property. Consequently, mortgage lenders may still insist on sending their own surveyor to the property in order to provide a valuation for mortgage purposes. A further problem is that the condition report will be much less comprehensive than the current RICS Home Buyers Reports. Consequently, many buyers will still want to commission their own structural survey.

Despite lobbying by professionals from within the property industry it now seems likely that the Home Information Pack will include a compulsory "condition report". If this happens it is likely that many mortgage lenders will drop their requirement for a separate valuation for mortgage purposes provided that the loan is less than say 90% of the property's value. They will rely instead upon an on-line valuation of the property based on the selling prices of similar houses nearby taken from Land Registry statistics.

Some buyers might be reluctant to accept a survey that was commissioned by the seller. The way round this would be to provide an insurance backed warranty that would compensate the buyer for the full cost of rectifying any defect that the surveyor missed. It is my opinion that market forces will lead to the introduction of such a system even if the 2007 legislation does not make it compulsory.

Some estate agency firms may try to pre-empt the Government's legislation by introducing their own voluntary Home Information Packs. The first of these are likely to be introduced from September 2005. However, until the vendor's surveyor is made legally accountable to the purchaser, such a survey will be of limited value and my advice would be to instruct your own surveyor before proceeding.

$$\left(10\right)$$

Consolidating the Sale

The present home buying process is horribly inefficient. The average time taken between the offer being agreed and the exchange of contracts is 12 weeks. Approximately 30 per cent of all the sales that are agreed fail to reach completion. This chapter will explain how to speed up the process and increase the chance of a satisfactory completion.

BUILDING A GOOD RELATIONSHIP WITH THE VENDORS
Love them or loathe them you have to try to maintain a satisfactory working relationship with your vendors until the sale reaches completion. The following hints will help you.

Confirming everything in writing
A great many problems are caused by misunderstandings. As soon as your offer is accepted, you should write to the agent to confirm all the details and conditions of the sale. A typical letter might look like the one in Figure 6.

The agent should also confirm to you details of the sale in writing. Check this letter carefully to make sure that there are no discrepancies with what you have previously agreed.

Arranging a consolidation visit
Last time you met the vendor you were adversaries. An excellent way to consolidate the sale is often to arrange to meet the vendors again in less adversarial circumstances.

Dear Mr Jones

Re: 1 Park Avenue, Anytown
SUBJECT TO CONTRACT

Further to my telephone conversation with the agent this morning I was delighted to hear that my offer to purchase the above property for the sum of £69,500 subject to contract has been accepted. I confirm the following details:

1. My offer is to include all carpets and all curtains in the ground floor rooms.

2. My offer is subject to the property being taken off the market immediately.

3. I am hoping to be able to exchange contracts within six weeks. My target completion date is 1st December.

4. I am applying for a 75% mortgage with the ABC Building Society. This is being arranged by XYZ Mortgage Brokers Limited, Tel: 12345 679010.

5. I shall be arranging for a home buyers survey on the property.

6. My solicitor is Mr G O Quickly, of Quickly and Company Solicitors, address and telephone number.

7. I have agreed a sale on my current property. My buyer, who is buying for the first time, has already carried out a survey and the result is satisfactory. The agent handling the sale is Mr Ivor Sale, of Sale and Company, address and telephone number.

8. I can be contacted if necessary on 123456 daytime and 7891011 evenings.

I hope this is an accurate summary of our agreement and I look forward to the purchase proceeding quickly and smoothly.

Yours sincerely

A Buyer

Fig. 6. Confirming acceptance of an offer.

The best bet is to think of a pretext which allows you to visit the property again, eg to measure for curtains or carpets. If you have a family, take them with you. During the visit tell the vendors how much you are looking forward to moving in and talk positively about what you are doing to expedite matters. The psychology behind this is that if you can establish a cordial relationship at the outset, you will be much better placed to resolve any difficulties that may arise later on.

Giving regular progress reports

It is vital to keep your vendors fully informed of all progress. Let them know as soon as:

◆ you have a date for a survey

◆ you receive a satisfactory survey result

◆ you receive a mortgage

◆ and whenever else a significant event occurs.

In any event try to keep in touch at least once a week. It is usually best to keep in touch with the estate agent rather than the vendors themselves unless you get on exceptionally well.

If a problem occurs, let the agent and/or the vendor know immediately. This will help to create an atmosphere of two parties who are working together to achieve a satisfactory outcome. It will also help to ensure that more time is available to resolve the issue.

The importance of speed

Above all else you need to exchange contracts as quickly as possible. There is a direct correlation between the length of time that the sale takes and the chances of it falling through. Every day of unnecessary delay is another day when things could go wrong. With this in mind most of the rest of this chapter is devoted to suggesting some things that you can do to speed matters up.

CASE STUDY
Marilyn gets a bargain by working fast

The flat that Marilyn P bought was an absolute bargain. The vendor, who was emigrating to New Zealand, had just lost a sale and was in a desperate hurry to sell quickly. He agreed to accept Marilyn's price provided that she could exchange contracts within 21 days.

Marilyn applied for a mortgage with the ABC Bank which her broker assured her had a reputation for swift service. She gave the bank written authority to go to survey before taking up references and, by ringing around, she found a surveyor who could visit the house the following day. Her broker told the bank that she was in a hurry and they pulled out all the stops. Five days later she had an offer of a mortgage.

Marilyn's solicitor was equally efficient. He came highly recommended and more than lived up to his reputation. Eleven days later Marilyn exchanged contracts.

Commenting on her experience, Marilyn says 'I spent hours running about to get everything done quickly, but it was certainly worth it. I love my new flat and I got it at an excellent price.'

TEN WAYS TO GET A QUICKER MORTGAGE OFFER

1. Choosing the mortgage lender

Choose your mortgage lender with care. The time it takes to deal with a mortgage application varies considerably from one lender to another. The quickest can give you a mortgage offer in ten days. The slowest often take four to six weeks. Check with your mortgage broker how long the mortgage offer is likely to take. If you are arranging a mortgage direct with the lender, ask them what their average turn-around is before you commit yourself.

2. Applying for a mortgage in principle

If you know which mortgage lender you wish to use you can often apply for a mortgage in principle before you find a property to buy. This means that the mortgage lender will take up employment and financial references and give you a certificate to say that they will lend you up to £X,000 subject to a satisfactory valuation on the property that you are buying. This can save seven to 14 days once you find a property (NB not all lenders offer a mortgage in principle).

3. Asking for the survey to be done first

Most mortgage lenders will not instruct the surveyor to carry out a mortgage valuation until they have obtained satisfactory financial and employment references. The reason for this is that they want to avoid wasting your survey fee if you are not creditworthy. The price, however, is a delay of seven to ten days.

The way to avoid this is to instruct the mortgage lender to proceed with the survey before obtaining references. This will usually have to be done in writing. A typical letter would read like the one in Figure 7.

4. Informing your employer

Mortgage applications are often delayed because employers are slow to respond, or respond to a reference request incorrectly. Find out which person in your organisation will be dealing with the reference and ensure that the lender sends it addressed to them by name. Go and see this person, and

---

Dear XYZ Building Society,

Re: 1 Park Avenue, Anytown

I am in a hurry to buy this property. In order to save time, I should be grateful if you would instruct the surveyor immediately, ie *before* obtaining references. I understand that if my references are not satisfactory, I will lose my survey fee but I am prepared to take this risk in order to obtain an early mortgage offer.

Yours sincerely

A Buyer

Fig. 7. Asking for the survey to be done first.

ask them to look out for the reference and return it immediately. Also make sure that they complete the mortgage lender's official reference request form. Most lenders will not accept the information in letter form.

5. Checking the lender's lending criteria

Many mortgages are turned down because the property does not meet the lender's criteria. If you are applying directly to the lender, or if your broker is not a mortgage specialist, ask for a copy of the lender's lending criteria and check that the property you are buying falls within them.

6. Doing your own credit check

If there is any possibility that you have a County Court Judgement for debt, ask your mortgage broker to do a credit check on you. If there is a problem, you can save the time that would be wasted if your loan application was refused and apply in the first case to a more appropriate mortgage lender.

7. Choosing the right surveyor

Before instructing a surveyor make sure that you ask how quickly they can get the report to you. Sometimes a surveyor will agree to do a report for you quickly in return for a higher fee.

8. Stressing the urgency

Mortgage lenders have been known to deal with applications within 48 hours. If you tell everyone that you are in a hurry, you might be surprised at what they can do to help.

9. Checking if a medical report is required

Most people who are arranging a mortgage will be applying for some sort of life assurance policy to cover the loan. If the loan is a large one (about £100,000 plus), or if you have ever had any medical problems, the insurance company might ask for a medical report. This could cause one to two week's delay. If there is any possibility that your insurer may require a medical report, ring their underwriting department and explain your circumstances. If a report is required, it can be arranged immediately. If you are arranging your loan through brokers they will usually do this for you.

10. Hassling people

If promised deadlines are not met, don't be frightened to complain loudly.

FOUR WAYS TO SAVE TIME ON THE LEGAL SIDE

1. Choosing the right solicitor

The importance of choosing the right solicitor cannot be over-emphasised. Get recommendations from your friends, the estate agent, the mortgage broker and the lending source. Speak to more than one firm before making a decision and never choose on price alone.

2. Instructing a solicitor as early as possible

If you are selling a property as well as buying, you should instruct a solicitor before you find a buyer. This will allow the solicitor to obtain the title deeds, prepare a draft contract, and prepare replies to standard precontract enquiries in readiness for the sale. This will save time once a buyer is found.

3. Applying for local authority searches

If you are confident of selling quickly, you might even ask your solicitor to apply for local searches. This could help to save several weeks. The drawback is that if the property does not sell quickly, the searches may go out of date which means that your search fee will have been wasted.

4. Checking what costs are involved

A great many sales fall through because the buyer underestimates the cost involved. However, do check with your solicitor that the costs which you allowed for are accurate in your case.

HOW NEW LEGISLATION MAY AFFECT THE PROCESS

If mortgage lenders drop their requirement for a mortgage valuation, they are likely to conduct even more stringent checks on the creditworthiness of borrowers. My prediction therefore is that it will become common practice for buyers to apply for a mortgage in principle before they start looking seriously for a property. In future, the process is likely to be:

◆ Buyer chooses a mortgage lender.

◆ Buyer applies for a mortgage in principle.

◆ Lender takes up financial and employment references.

◆ Lender grants mortgage in principle.

◆ Buyer finds property.

◆ Lender studies survey report commissioned by vendor.

◆ Lender conducts an on-line search of actual prices of similar properties in the area with the Land Registry.

◆ Lender makes unconditional mortgage offer.

This process would allow a mortgage offer to be made within a few days of the offer being accepted.

$$\left(11\right)$$

Taking Action When Things Go Wrong

Under the present home buying system one in three of all sales fails to reach completion.

By following the advice given in previous chapters, you will significantly reduce the odds of your purchase going wrong.

However, nothing can guarantee that your purchase will be trouble-free. This chapter describes some of the more common problems which you may experience and gives advice on how to resolve them.

I have divided the problem into three areas.

Estate agency problems

◆ Gazumping
◆ Vendor decides not to sell
◆ Problems with the chain.

Mortgage problems

◆ Property does not meet lending criteria
◆ Delayed employment references
◆ Unsatisfactory employment references

◆ Mortgage refused
◆ County Court judgement for debt
◆ Poor credit references
◆ Failed credit scoring
◆ Not on the electoral register
◆ Late survey
◆ Property down-valued on survey
◆ Survey reveals repairs needed
◆ Retention notice made
◆ Total retention
◆ Damp report required
◆ Timber report required
◆ Structural engineer's report required
◆ Property is uninsurable
◆ Later mortgage offer
◆ Medical report required
◆ Life cover refused.

Legal problems

◆ Slow/pedantic solicitor
◆ Delays in obtaining title deeds
◆ Delay in obtaining office copy entries
◆ Unregistered title
◆ Delay in receiving draft contracts
◆ Disputes over terms of the contract
◆ Delays in obtaining local searches
◆ Delays in answering preliminary enquiries
◆ Boundary disputes
◆ Restrictive covenants
◆ Planning and building regulations problems
◆ Fixtures and fittings

♦ Insufficient funds to exchange
♦ Use of deposit by vendor
♦ Arguments over completion dates
♦ Short lease
♦ Defective lease
♦ Unpaid service charges.

AVOIDING BEING GAZUMPED

Of all the things that can go wrong **gazumping** is the one that raises the fiercest passions.

What is gazumping?

Gazumping means a vendor reneging on their agreement to sell you a property at a certain price. For example, a property is for sale at an asking price of £99,950. You make an offer of £95,000 which the vendor accepts. A few hours, days or even weeks later, a second buyer makes an offer of £96,000 for the same property. The vendor rings you and says:

A. I'm selling to someone else for more money or
B. Unless you increase your offer to £96,000 or more I will sell to somebody else.

In both cases you have been gazumped. Gazumping is *not* the acceptance of an offer above the asking price. In order to gazump you a vendor has to renege on an offer after it has been accepted. Thus, if a property is for sale at £99,950 and two buyers bid against each other until a sale is agreed at £105,000, the losing party has not been gazumped. They have just been outbid.

How common is gazumping?

Gazumping is not nearly as common as the press would have us believe. It affects only about one to two per cent of all transactions, and occurs mostly in London and the south east where the market is most buoyant. Nevertheless, when it does occur it is most unpleasant. The gazumped buyer is caused considerable inconvenience, and is often left with a bill for legal fees and survey fees of several hundred pounds.

Why does it happen?

Gazumping usually occurs because a property is kept on the market after a sale has been agreed. Sometimes there is a legitimate reasons for the vendor to do this: for example, the buyer has not yet sold their own property. In other cases, the vendor is dissatisfied with the original offer and keeps the property on the market to try to obtain a higher one.

Gazumping is most likely to happen when a sale is slow to progress in a buoyant market, where prices can sometimes rise by as much as two or three per cent per month. Thus a property that is sold for £100,000 could be worth as much as £109,000 by the time a slow purchaser is ready to exchange contracts 12 weeks later.

Whose fault is it?

Estate agents are usually held responsible for gazumping. In truth, they are not usually the guilty party. An estate agent has a legal and ethical duty to act in accordance with the client's instructions at all times. Thus if a client tells him to keep the property on the market after an offer has been accepted, then he must do so. If a higher offer is received, the agent must by law pass it on to the vendor. The decision to gazump someone is always made by the vendor, not by the agent. The real culprit, though, is the outdated home buying process which causes an average delay of eight weeks before contracts can be exchanged.

How can you avoid being gazumped?

There are five things you can do to reduce the chances of being gazumped.

◆ Do not try to buy a property until you have sold your own.
◆ Insist that the property you are buying is taken off the market as a condition of your offer.
◆ Exchange contracts as quickly as possible.
◆ Keep the vendor closely informed of all progress.
◆ Try to maintain a cordial relationship with the vendor throughout.

CASE STUDY
Bill mistakenly tries to negotiate a reduction

Bill C agreed to buy a two-bedroomed luxury flat in Bournemouth for £95,000. The vendor accepted Bill's offer but said that he would leave the property on the market just in case something went wrong. Three weeks later Bill received his survey report. The property had been down-valued to £90,000 due to the need to replace the old-fashioned kitchen and bathroom. Bill sent a copy of the survey to his vendor and asked for a £5,000 reduction in the purchase price.

His vendor responded with fury. Much of his reply is unrepeatable but the gist of it was that Bill could have seen the state of the kitchen and bathroom for himself, that the flat was worth £95,000 and that if Bill didn't want to buy it a queue of other people did.

Bill was a bit taken aback by this but on reflection decided that he did want to continue with his purchase. When he informed his vendor of this the following day he met with another barrage of abuse. Apparently the vendor had now agreed to sell to another party at £98,000 and was no longer prepared to consider Bill's offer.

Commenting on his experience, Bill says, 'I shall never know whether the vendor was intending to gazump me and used the survey report as an excuse or whether he reacted badly because he thought I was trying it on. With hindsight the flat was worth £95,000 and I wish I had not tried to negotiate a reduction. I shall almost certainly have to pay more for another flat like it.'

HANDLING THE VENDOR WHO NO LONGER WANTS TO SELL

A simple change of mind by either party is the single most common cause of sales falling through. However, it is comparatively rare for someone to change their mind for no reason at all. The way to deal with vendors who change their minds about selling to you is to find out *why* they have done so. Ask the estate agent why. If you can't get a satisfactory answer, try ringing the vendors yourself. Very often you will find that the reason is because their mortgage application was turned down or they received an adverse survey report on the property that they were buying. If you can find out what the real problem is you may be able to solve it.

Problems with the chain

All the problems highlighted in this section can also affect other people up and down the chain. If you suspect this to be the case, you may have to do a little detective work of your own by ringing other agents, purchasers or vendors to establish what the problem is. A common frustration is that some estate agents do not spend as much time on sales progressing as they should do. Some do not even check out the chain with the proper degree of care. In a long chain you may have to find one good agent going up the chain and one good agent going down the chain and rely upon them to help you locate where the problems lie.

OVERCOMING 20 COMMON MORTGAGE PROBLEMS
1 Property does not meet lending criteria

If your application is turned down for this reason, you have two choices. You can appeal for the mortgage lender to make an exception; a more senior person may have authority to bend the rules. The only alternative is to reapply to a different lender. In either case you will suffer a significant delay.

2 Delayed employment references

Most lenders will not carry out the survey until they have obtained satisfactory employment references. You may be able to speed things up by asking the lender to carry out the survey before they receive references. If you do this, bear in mind that you will lose your survey fee if your references are not satisfactory.

3 Unsatisfactory employment references

The most common problem is when part of the earnings are paid as overtime, commission or bonus and the employer will not guarantee them. This means that the lender will only allow half their value for mortgage purposes. The way to avoid the problem is to check whether your employer will guarantee your bonuses before the application is submitted. Once the problem has occurred you may be able to persuade the lender to make an exception in your case, but the most likely outcome is that you will have to apply to a different mortgage lender.

4 Mortgage refused

If your mortgage is refused because the property does not meet the lender's criteria, or for some other practical reasons, the lender will normally say so. If the application is refused without explana-tion, it probably means that there is a problem with your credit-worthiness.

5 County Court Judgements

You may have a County Court Judgement registered against you of which you are unaware because it was registered at a previous address. If you suspect that this may be the case, the way to check is to ask the mortgage lender to provide you with the name and address of the credit referencing agent which it used. You can then write to the agency and demand to see a copy of your own file (it costs £2). If you do have a CCJ it will be extremely difficult to persuade the lender to make the loan to you no matter what the circumstances. However, once you are aware of the problem, you can appeal against the judgement if you feel it to be unjust and/or declare it on any future mortgage applications.

Although a CCJ will limit your choice of mortgage lender, many mainstream lenders will lend provided that the CCJ is satisfied (fully paid) and declared on their application form. If you have more than one CCJ, you will probably have to apply to a lender which specialises in impaired credit cases. This may mean that you have to pay more for your loan.

6 Poor credit references

Your loan may be turned down if other current or previous occupants of your current property have a poor credit history. For example, your adult son may have run up debts before he left home. The way to discover this is to apply for your own credit file as described above.

If you can prove that you have no connection with the other party, you may be able to persuade the lender to reconsider their decision. You can also place your own 'correction statement' on the credit record explaining the situation. This should help to prevent similar problems occurring in the future.

7 Failed credit scoring

If there is nothing adverse in your credit reference, the most likely explanation for your loan being refused is that you have failed the lender's credit scoring procedure. The way that credit scoring works is described in Chapter 4. You can appeal against the lender's decision but the chances of success are not good. The best bet is probably to reapply to a different lender.

If you are using a mortgage broker, they will probably have a pretty good idea about why your loan was refused. They may be able to help you to decide which lender to apply to next time.

8 Not on the Electoral Register

The mortgage lender will be very suspicious if you are not on the Electoral Register at your current address. If you are not on it, you should make the lender or the broker aware of this at the time that you make your mortgage application. You will almost certainly have to produce evidence of your residency in the form of, for example, utility bills. Some lenders will require an affidavit (a sworn statement) from a professional person, for example your doctor. Some lenders will turn your application down out of hand if you are not on the Electoral Register.

9 Late survey

The survey should be carried out within ten to 14 days of submitting the mortgage application. It is important that the survey is carried out promptly because it is the first sign that the vendor has that your mortgage application is proceeding. If the survey is late, the most likely reason is a problem with your financial or employment references. The other possibility is inefficiency on behalf of the lender and/or the surveyor.

The best way to avoid delays here is to ask the surveyor to commit to a date when he will be able to carry out the survey, and a date when he will be able to submit the final report, *before* you instruct him. If the survey is not carried out on this date, you can telephone to complain. If the surveyor cannot carry out the survey within a satisfactory timescale, your last resort is to cancel your instructions and instruct another (less busy) surveyor.

10 Property down-valued on survey

It is quite common to find that the surveyor's valuation for mortgage purposes is less than the agreed purchase price. There are several things that you can do to avoid this problem from occurring.

◆ Instruct a surveyor with up-to-date knowledge of local values.

◆ Provide the surveyor with particulars of any comparable properties which you have relied upon to form your own opinion of value.

◆ Choose your surveyor with care – some have a reputation for over-cautious valuation.

◆ If you are applying for a high-percentage mortgage, let the surveyor know that the valuation is critical at the time that you instruct him or her.

If despite these precautions the property is still down-valued, you will have to make a decision on whether you are able to/still wish to proceed.

CASE STUDY
Stan negotiates a better price

Stan B was buying a three-bedroomed house in Swansea for his son who had just secured a university place there. The house was an ordinary house in a rather run-down part of the town, but it was better and cheaper than student digs and Stan felt that it would be a good investment.

The property was down-valued on survey from £45,000 to £40,000 because of dampness, wiring problems and problems with the roof. Stan sent the agent a copy of his survey report together with a letter making a revised offer of £40,000. The vendor was reluctant to accept this.

Stan checked to make sure that similar properties were available, then sent another letter to the agent mentioning that another property was now for sale in the road for £38,000 and that the vendor could take his offer or leave it. The vendor accepted the revised offer.

Commenting on his tactics Stan says 'I was in a strong negotiating position because I knew that I could walk away. There were plenty of other properties available, and the market was fairly stagnant. With hindsight I could probably have bought the house for £38,000.'

Assessing if you can afford to proceed

If you are applying for a 95 per cent mortgage from a lender that will not lend more than 95 per cent of the purchase price, any down-valuation will mean that you will have to find money from elsewhere in order to increase your deposit. For example:

Agreed price	£100,000
95 per cent mortgage advance	£95,000
Deposit required	£5,000
Surveyor values property at	£95,000
Maximum advance is therefore	
95 per cent × £95,000	£90,250
Deposit required	£9,750

You may be able to persuade your vendor to accept a corresponding reduction in the purchase price. If not, unless you can find another £4,750 you will not be able to proceed.

You may be able to arrange a top-up loan from another source but this is likely to be expensive. However, some mortgage lenders will not allow you to borrow the further money elsewhere for fear that it may compromise their security. If you still want to proceed with your purchase, the only alternative is to apply to another mortgage lender and hope that a different surveyor values the property at the full purchase price.

If the mortgage that you are applying for is below the lender's maximum loan to valuation, you will not have to find the extra money in cash. The lender will simply increase the percentage loan. For example:

Purchase price	£100,000
Loan	£70,000
Deposit	£30,000
Loan to valuation ratio is	70 per cent
Property valued at	£90,000
Loan	£70,000
Loan to valuation is £70,000 ÷ £90,000	77.7 per cent

A point to bear in mind is that in this example, the new loan is above 75 per cent of the valuation. This means that some lenders would charge a mortgage indemnity premium (see Chapter 2). This could increase the cost of loan by several hundred pounds.

Deciding if you still want to proceed

Once you have determined whether you can afford to proceed, you have to decide whether you still wish to do so. The first thing to do is to make your own value judgement. Do you still think the property is worth the purchase price agreed? Having decided this, your exact course of action will depend upon a number of factors.

◆ If you are buying a highly desirable property in a buoyant market, and you believe the property to be worth the price agreed, the best course of action might be to proceed without mentioning the down-valuation to the vendor. Your chance of securing a price reduction may be slight and any attempt to do so could jeopardise your purchase.

◆ If the property is less desirable or the market less buoyant, you might want to use the survey report to try

Dear Mr Jones

Re: 1 Park Avenue, Anytown
SUBJECT TO CONTRACT

I am sorry to inform you that my surveyor has valued the property at £90,000. This is £10,000 less than the agreed purchase price. I am enclosing a copy of the report. I have challenged my surveyor over his valuation but he has defended it by citing several comparable properties, particularly No. 7 which has just been sold for £90,000.

In the light of this I feel that I must revise my offer to £90,000. I still hope that the sale will be able to continue and I look forward to hearing from you with your comments.

Yours sincerely

A Buyer

Fig. 8. Negotiating a reduction.

Dear Mr Jones

Re: 1 Park Avenue, Anytown
SUBJECT TO CONTRACT

I am so sorry that we were unable to reach an agreement on a revised purchase price. For the reasons stated I am not prepared to pay more than £92,500. I am now looking for an alternative property but I should like to buy yours. Please let me know if you change your mind.

Yours sincerely

A Buyer

Fig. 9. A withdrawal letter.

to negotiate a reduction in the purchase price. If so, it is well worth telephoning the surveyor and asking how they arrived at the valuation. You can use these arguments to support your case. It is usually best to handle these negotiations in writing. A typical letter might look like the one in Figure 8.

If the vendors refuse to budge at all or are only prepared to concede part of the differential, you will have to make a decision on whether to proceed or not. This should be based not on the surveyor's valuation, but on how easy it will be to buy a similar property for the same or a lower amount. You should also consider the amount of inconvenience that you would suffer if you withdrew from the purchase.

If you do withdraw, always leave the door open for the future. It is surprising how many vendors call your bluff then call back 24 hours later and say that they will accept the lower offer after all. You need to make it easy for your vendor to do this without losing face. A typical withdrawal letter might read like the one in Figure 9.

11 Survey reveals repairs needed

If the survey reveals repairs are needed, you will need to renegotiate the purchase price using similar principles to those set out above. Before you quantify your request you will need to separate out the work highlighted in the survey into three separate categories.

◆ Faults that have been allowed for in the price.
◆ Faults that you could have spotted yourself.
◆ Faults that you could not have spotted yourself.

If the need to replace the roof was discussed before the offer was made you can hardly expect the vendor to agree to another reduction to reflect the cost of this. If you complain that the windows need painting, the vendor may reasonably point out that you could have noticed this for yourself and allowed for it in your original offer. The third category of faults may warrant a reduction.

Estimating the costs

Before you make a request for a reduction you need to make sure that you have an accurate idea of the likely cost of the

---

Dear Mr Jones

Re: 1 Park Avenue, Anytown
SUBJECT TO CONTRACT

I have just received my survey report which I am afraid has revealed a number of problems.

- The damp course needs replacing, estimated cost £2,500.
- The garden wall is dangerous and needs rebuilding, estimated cost £1,000.
- The heating system does not function property, estimated cost £2,000.

All the above matters require urgent attention and in view of this I must reduce my offer from £95,000 to £90,000 to reflect the cost of the work.

I still very much want to proceed with my purchase and I hope that this revised offer will be acceptable to you.

I am enclosing a copy of my survey report.

Yours sincerely

A Buyer

Fig. 10. Requesting a reduction.

necessary work. For this you cannot rely on the survey report. Most surveyors are general practice surveyors. This means that they can identify most faults but will not necessarily have an up-to-date idea of the cost of rectifying them. If the work required is extensive, it may be worth getting a builder's estimate before you commence negotiations. If the work required is very extensive you may need to commission a quantity surveyor to prepare a detailed estimate.

It is usually best to make your request for a reduction in writing. A typical letter is shown in Figure 10.

Deciding whether to proceed

If the vendor will not agree to reduce by the whole amount, you will need to take a decision on whether or not to proceed. As before, this decision should take into account the ease with which you are likely to be able to find an alternative property and the inconvenience that pulling out of the sale would cause to you and your family.

12 Retention notice made

If a defect is minor, the surveyor will merely point it out. If it is more serious, the lender may ask you to give an undertaking that you will complete the necessary repairs within, say, six months. In practice mortgage lenders seldom check to see whether you have actually done so.

If the defect is very serious, the lender may make a **retention**. This means that they will retain a certain sum until the repairs have been carried out. The problem is that if the lender retains £5,000 to cover the cost of fixing the roof, where do you get the money from to fix the roof? The solution is to go to your own bank and arrange a short-term loan. The bank may require an undertaking from your solicitor to repay the loan out of the mortgage advance when it is released. This type of loan is fairly easy to arrange, but it will take a week or so to organise and this could cause delay.

The way to avoid this is to ring the mortgage lender a day or two after the survey took place and ask if the surveyor has found any major defects. If so, you need to ask whether they intend to make a retention. By making this phone call, you will find out about the problem sooner and have more time to arrange a temporary loan.

13 Total retention

When the defect is very serious, the lender may retain the entire mortgage advance until repairs have been completed. The process for dealing with this is described above. However, a larger loan will take longer to arrange.

CASE STUDY
Hilary overcomes a retention clause

Hilary M made an offer to buy a two-bedroomed Victorian cottage in south east London. The property was in a terrible state but Hilary felt the price agreed reflected this. The survey revealed the problems that she had expected and valued the property at the full purchase price. However, in view of the severity of the problems, the lender said that it would hold back

£30,000 of the £70,000 mortgage advance until the problems had been rectified.

On the advice of her mortgage broker Hilary went to her bank and negotiated a £30,000 loan to fund the shortfall. Her solicitor gave an undertaking to repay this out of the proceeds of the mortgage advance when it was released.

Commenting on her experience, Hilary says, 'When I read the mortgage offer and saw the £30,000 retention, I thought that was the end of it. Fortunately my broker knew what to do. I am delighted with my property and now the work is finished it is probably worth at least £20,000 more than I paid for it. It was an excellent buy.'

14 Damp report required

The surveyor will often ask for a damp report. The way to prevent this from causing delay is to telephone the surveyor the day after they visit the property. Ask if there are any major problems and whether they will be asking for any supplementary reports.

If they have recommended a damp report, you will have extra time to arrange one. The estate agent will probably be able to recommend a company who can carry out a report. For the reasons stated in Chapter 9, you should treat their recommendations with suspicion.

15 Timber report required

If the property that you are buying is an older one and does not have current timber guarantees, the surveyor may ask for a timber report. The process for dealing with this is the same as for the damp report. Many companies undertake both damp and timber treatment and will produce a com-bined report.

16 Structural engineer's report required

If the property shows any signs of subsidence or has a history of subsidence, the valuer may ask for a structural engineer's report. Often this is just a precautionary measure. However, the consequences of subsidence can be so serious that many buyers run a mile at the mere mention of the word.

Having got this far it is probably worth paying for the structural engineer to visit the property before you pull out. Their visit may entirely alleviate your fears. If the property does have subsidence it may prove extremely difficult to resell and even if your mortgage lender is prepared to lend on the property you should think carefully about proceeding.

17 Property is uninsurable

If a property has ever suffered from subsidence, if it has ever flooded or it is located in a flood plain it may be difficult to obtain building insurance even after the necessary repairs have been carried out. If you are buying such a property, the easiest solution is often to take over the current buildings policy from the present owner..

Be warned, though. The cost of insurance may be much

more than usual. You should therefore obtain a quote before committing yourself, and possibly negotiate a reduction in the purchase price sufficient to compensate you for the high cost of future premiums.

18 Late mortgage offer

One of the commonest problems of all is delays in receiving the final mortgage offer. Until you have got this you cannot exchange contracts. This problem can be largely avoided by choosing a mortgage lender with a reputation for speed and efficiency of service. Unfortunately this may mean a trade-off with the mortgage rate. A mortgage lender that is offering a particularly attractive rate is likely to receive more applications than usual. This often leads to delays in under-writing cases. You will need to make your own decision on this, but bear in mind that a mortgage which is a quarter of a per cent cheaper will be of little use to you if you end up losing the property that you are trying to buy.

All mortgage lenders experience peaks and troughs in the number of mortgage applications that they receive, and you may just be unlucky or apply during a particularly busy period. If you do not receive a mortgage offer within seven days of the survey being carried out, telephone the mortgage lender or your broker to find out whether there is a specific problem that is holding things up. If not, find out the name of the person who is responsible for getting your mortgage offer out and badger them every day until you receive it.

19 Medical report required

If you are applying for any sort of life assurance policy as part of your mortgage application, the insurer may need a medical report. This usually happens when the policy applied for is particularly large (usually about £100,000 plus) or if there is anything adverse in your medical history (eg a close relative who has had a heart attack).

A medical report typically takes seven to ten days to arrange. If one is necessary, you need to know as soon as possible in order to avoid it causing an unnecessary delay. If you suspect that a medical report may be required in your case, ring the life assurance company and ask them.

20 Life cover refused

If your medical history is very poor, your life policy may be refused. In this case you need to approach a specialist independent insurance broker who has experience in impaired life 'cases'. Even if your health is very poor most risks are insurable at a price. If your broker does not have the experience necessary to arrange such a policy, ask them to recommend one who does.

OVERCOMING THE MOST COMMON LEGAL PROBLEMS
1 Slow/pedantic solicitor

The importance of choosing a solicitor with care has already been emphasised. Once you have chosen a solicitor it is extremely difficult to change to another one. By the time you have arranged for all the documents to be returned, you would have wasted at least seven to ten days. Changing solicitors half-way through is not to be recommended except in the most extreme of circumstances.

If your solicitor fails to live up to your expectations all you can do is to badger and cajole them into action. Never forget that you are the customer.

2 Delays in obtaining title deeds

The vendor's solicitor cannot prepare the draft contract until they have the title deeds. If the property that you are buying is mortgaged, these will usually be held by the vendor's mortgage lender. If the vendors own the property outright, the title deeds may be held for safe keeping by their previous mortgage lender, their bank or solicitor. On the other hand they may have fallen down behind the piano.

It is reasonable to allow the vendor's solicitor seven to ten days to obtain the title deeds. Ask your solicitor or the estate agent to check that they have been obtained within this timescale. If not, get thevendors to chase up their mortgage lender and/or solicitor.

If the deeds have been lost, the vendors will have to re-prove their title to the property. This could cause considerable delay. In such cases you might do well to consider finding an alternative property.

3 Delay in obtaining office copy entries

If the property that you are buying has registered title, the vendors' solicitor will apply for office copy entries of the title from the Land Registry. These must be obtained before the draft contract can be prepared. Some solicitors do not apply for office copy entries until a week or two into the sale in order to avoid incurring a fee if the sale fails to proceed for any reason. This will cause delays later on. Unless you have good cause to doubt whether the sale is going to proceed, you should check with your solicitor that office copy entries have been requested during the first progress call.

4 Unregistered title

There are two systems of land conveyancing in England and Wales. In the registered system, title to the land is registered at the Land Registry and guaranteed by the state. Disputes over title are therefore rare.

In the unregistered system, title is not registered with or guaranteed by the state. It must be proved by checking details of all previous conveyances. Disputes are therefore much more common and can become protracted. If you are buying an unregistered property and there is any dispute over the vendor's title, the best advice might be to abandon your purchase and seek an alternative property.

5 Delay in receiving draft contracts

Solicitors should receive a draft contract within a couple of weeks. If not, you need to investigate the cause of the delay. It could be that the vendors' solicitor is waiting for the title deeds or office copy entries. It could be that the solicitor has all the necessary documents but has been slow to produce the contract. In either event you should ring the agent or the vendors and ask them to chivvy things along.

6 Disputes over the terms of the contract

The draft contract is the document that sets out the terms of the sale. Most of the clauses are standard or semi-standard and come straight form a word processor. These are seldom contentious. The problem arises when a non-standard clause is introduced and its inclusion or exclusion turns into a battle of wills between the solicitors.

If you are told that your purchase is being held up due to difficulty in agreeing the terms of the contract, you should insist that your solicitor explains in layman's terms what the relevant clause covers and what the dispute is about. Very often a quick chat with the vendors or their agent will facilitate resolution of the problem.

7 Delays in obtaining local searches

Some local authorities are notoriously slow at responding to search enquiries. In order to avoid delays later on, it is essential to check that your solicitor has applied for a search immediately. However, often even this isn't soon enough and the absence of a local search ends up being the only thing that prevents contracts being exchanged.

In such circumstances the best solution might be to arrange a personal search. This means that someone (a member of staff from your own solicitors or a professional search agent) will visit the council in person to obtain the information that the council is too busy to provide. You will have to pay for the time involved. You will also have to buy an insurance policy to protect against the consequences of anything being missed. The total cost might be three or four times as much as the usual search fee but it is worth it if it prevents you from losing your property.

8 Delays in answering preliminary enquiries

Your solicitor will submit a long list of questions to the vendors' solicitor. These questions will cover issues such as:

◆ boundaries and any disputes relating to them

◆ covenants and easements

◆ mains services

◆ guarantees for work carried out

◆ NHBC certificate if the property is new

◆ planning matters

◆ fixtures and fittings.

The full list of questions looks quite intimidating, but in fact many of the questions are standard and many of the answers are 'I do not know' or 'Rely upon your own enquiries'. If there is a delay in providing this information, you will need to check whether the vendor has failed to supply the necessary information or whether the solicitor has not passed it on. Some questions tend to cause a disproportionate amount of problems (see next four sections).

9 Boundary disputes

If your vendor has ever had a dispute over boundaries or fences with any of their neighbours, your solicitor will probably advise you to run a mile. The consequences of a boundary dispute are regularly featured in television 'neighbours from hell' documentaries. One of the worst cases I know involved a farmer and his neighbour in Oxford-shire who were arguing over a strip of land 18 inches wide and 90 feet long. Between them they ran up legal costs of over £100,000. The farmer lost and ended up forfeiting the land and paying the legal costs of both sides. For the same sum, the farmer could have bought about 30 acres of land anywhere else in Oxfordshire.

If you are determined to proceed with the purchase regardless, you would be advised to try to meet the neighbour concerned to try to ensure that the dispute does not recur.

10 Restrictive covenants

Restrictive covenants fall into two categories: those that have already been broken and those that have not. For example, suppose that you are buying a five-year-old property on an estate. The builder may have put a convenant on all properties that forbids the addition of any extensions without his approval. The reason for this is to ensure that the estate is not disfigured by ugly extensions.

If you are planning to add a conservatory after you buy the property, you would have to approach the developer to ask permission. Most developers charge an administration fee to consider your application. If it is rejected, you would have to take a view on whether you still wished to proceed with the purchase.

Much more serious problems are caused when a covenant has already been breached. Suppose that you are buying a Victorian property with the same convenant preventing extensions being built, but in this instance an extension has already been added to the property. It might be impossible to track down the developer who built the house 100 years ago to ask for permission retrospectively. However, there is a risk that the builder's successors could at some future time try to enforce the covenant. If they did, it may mean demolition of the extension. The solution to this type of problem is to buy an insurance policy that protects against the risk of loss should a covenant be enforced. Because the risk of most convenants being enforced is slight, premiums tend to be relatively modest. It normally takes a couple of weeks to arrange such a policy.

11 Planning and building regulation problems

If the property that you are buying has an extension added, your solicitor will need to check that it has the appropriate planning and building regulation consents.

If it has not, it may be necessary to apply for these retro-spectively. This could cause lengthy delays. Indeed, the council might refuse to give consent and insist that the extension in question is demolished. If you run into problems of this nature, it may be best to look for another property.

The way to avoid such problems is to ask the owner or their estate agent three questions *before* you make an offer.

◆ Have you ever added an extension to the property?

◆ If so did you apply for planning consent?

◆ Did you get building regulation approval?

Asking these questions at the outset could save a great deal of time, money and frustration later on.

CASE STUDY
Building regulations hold up Petra's purchase

The present owner of the property which Petra K was buying had built a small extension onto his kitchen nine months before. The extension was so small that planning permission had not been required. Unfortunately the extension still needed building regulation approval and the vendor had failed to apply for this.

The first that Petra knew of the problem was when her solicitor received replies to preliminary enquiries. Petra' solicitor warned her to abandon her purchase at that point, but as it was such a pretty cottage she did not want to give up without a fight.

The vendor applied to the council for retrospective approval. They sent a building inspector to look at the extension and he made pages of notes about items that might not comply with current regulations. The correspondence went back and forth for 14 weeks until the council was eventually satisfied. In the meanwhile Petra was forced to take unpleasant and temporary accommodation.

Commenting on her experience, Petra says, 'I should have taken my solicitor's advice to withdraw as soon as the problem arose. I have been put to considerable inconvenience, but at least I got the property in the end. I might have waited 14 weeks only to find that the council insisted on demolishing half the kitchen.'

12 Fixtures and fittings

Fixtures and fittings cause more arguments than anything else. I know of many cases where an argument over a washing line, a toothbrush holder or a quarter of a tank of heating oil has jeopardised a sale. Don't let it happen to you. A detailed list of what is and is not included should be agreed in writing through the estate agents at the time that the offer is agreed and confirmed by the solicitors. If a dispute over a trivial item does blow up, don't be stubborn. It may be humiliating to let your vendor get away with digging up the rose bush in the front garden, but it is not worth pulling out of the sale over.

13 Insufficient funds to exchange

Many purchasers underestimate the costs that they will incur when buying a property. Make sure that you obtain a detailed estimate of all the costs that you will incur on day one. Your estate agent, mortgage broker or solicitor will all be pleased to do this for you.

A particular problem occurs when buyers are obtaining a mortgage for more than 90 per cent of the purchase price. In such circumstances most solicitors will accept a reduced deposit on exchange of contracts, but some will not. If this is the case, you will need to know as soon as possible so that you can arrange an alternative loan for the balance.

Finally remember that your solicitor will not exchange contracts until your cheque to fund the deposit has cleared. Either arrange a banker's draft or ensure that your solicitor has your cheque at least seven days before exchange of contracts is due to occur.

CASE STUDY
Martin's inefficient solicitor creates problems

Martin S had been unhappy with his solicitors almost from the outset. The nice chap who gave him the quote was always too busy to speak to him and he had little confidence in his assistant. The final straw came two days before exchange of contracts was due to take place. Martin's solicitor rang to tell him that his vendor's solicitor would not take a reduced deposit. Martin would have to find another £5,000 before he could exchange.

Martin was furious. Surely this problem could have been discovered weeks ago. Why had it not been mentioned before? His solicitor could give no satisfactory explanation. Fortunately Martin was able to arrange a bank loan for the balance, but it cost him nearly £200 and it delayed exchange of contracts for a week. His vendor was furious and he nearly lost the property.

Commenting on his experience, Martin says, 'This problem could easily have been predicted. I am still cross that I was not told about the problems sooner. I shall certainly not use that firm of solicitors again.'

14 Use of deposit by vendor

Most solicitors will allow the purchaser's deposit to be passed up the chain to fund the vendors' own purchase.

However, some solicitors won't allow their client's deposit

to be used in this way because there is a small risk that it could be lost. The way to avoid problems here is to ask your solicitor early on in the sale whether they will allow your deposit to be used to fund the vendors' deposit on their purchase. If not, you need to warn your vendor about this in good time so that they can make alternative arrangements.

15 Arguments over completion dates

Many chains break down because the parties involved cannot agree on a completion date. There are three things that you can do to avoid problems here. The first is to let everyone know your target completion from the very outset. The second is to be aware that completion dates do not have to be 28 days. They can be as short or as long as the parties wish them to be. Sometimes a simultaneous exchange and completion suits everyone best. On other occasions, an extended completion period of perhaps three or six months can give all parties the best combination of early certainty and sufficient time to make their personal arrangements.

Finally don't dismiss the option of moving into temporary accommodation or even taking a bridging loan. If contracts have been exchanged, the risk of things going wrong is very slight. The cost of moving twice might be less than the cost of withdrawing from the purchase.

SPECIAL PROBLEMS WITH LEASEHOLD PROPERTIES
1 Short lease

If the lease has less than about 70 years left to run, you may have difficulty in reselling the property (except in central London). If you are buying such a property, it is a sensible precaution to enquire about the cost of buying a lease extension as early as possible in the transaction. If the cost is prohibitive, you may wish to reconsider your decision to proceed with purchase.

If a leaseholder and a freeholder cannot agree upon a fair price for the lease renewal it is usually possible for the leaseholder to appeal to the Land Tribunal. It will calculate a fair value for the lease extension and can compel the freeholder to grant it at this price. The legislation and the accompanying valuation formula is complex and some properties are exempt so it is essential to take professional advice on this before proceeding.

2 Defective lease

A lot of the flats that were converted from large houses during the 1970s and 80s suffer from badly drafted leases. A typical problem would be failure to define clearly who is responsible for maintaining the common parts. If the defect in the lease is serious, your solicitor might advise you not to proceed unless you are able to obtain a Deed of Variation. This means getting the freeholder's permission to change the original terms of the lease. Negotiations over this could become quite protracted and there is no guarantee of success. If you are in a hurry to buy, the best thing might be to find another property.

3 Unpaid service charges

Responsibility for maintaining the building often rests with the landlord. Some landlords collect substantial service charges every year but fail to carry out any maintenance work. In such circumstances leaseholders sometimes stop paying the service charge. This is most unwise. The law in this area is very one-sided. It is extremely difficult for leaseholders to force their landlords to undertake maintenance work, but the sanctions that landlords can employ against leaseholders who fail to pay their service charges are draconian.

However unfair it may seem, your vendor will have to pay all charges up to date before they can sell their flat. If the landlord has a very poor history of maintaining the building, you may wish to reconsider your decision to buy the property.

New legislation now means that it is usually possible for leaseholders to take over management of their own block with or without the freeholder's consent. However, legislation in this area is complex and some properties are exempt. You will need to take professional advice on this before proceeding.

HOW NEW LEGISLATION MAY AFFECT THE PROCESS

The proposed introduction of a compulsory Home Information Pack could have a very beneficial effect on the home buying process. By making more information available form the outset average transaction times would be reduced considerably and many of the problems highlighted in this section could be avoided.

Further legislation is also planned to redress the imbalance between freeholders' and leaseholders' rights. In future, leaseholders may have the right to acquire the freehold of their building and to take over management of it if their freeholder fails to provide an efficient service.

$$\left(12\right)$$

Preparing for the Move

This chapter explains what you need to do to ensure that the move itself goes smoothly.

PREPARING FOR EXCHANGE OF CONTRACTS

You will know that exchange of contracts is imminent when your solicitor asks to arrange an appointment to sign the contract. Although this is certainly a good sign, do not relax just yet. Things can and do go wrong at the very last minute. Two problems in particular arise more often than most.

Arguments over completion dates

Even at this late stage sales can and do break down because the parties involved are unable to agree on a completion date. The things that you can do to defuse this problem are explained in Chapter 11.

Gazumping

A really heartless vendor may try to gazump you on the very day that you are due to exchange contracts. He knows that at this point you will have invested the maximum amount of time, money and emotion into planning your move and sees this as an excellent negotiating opportunity.

It is hard to know what to advise if this happens to you. Your natural reaction will be to tell your vendor to forget the whole thing, but in a buoyant market it may prove impossible to buy a similar house for the same price. In addition to any financial loss you need to take account of the emotional cost and inconvenience that would be caused if you have to start all over again. There are certain circumstances where the best thing to do is to swallow your pride and pay the extra money.

CASE STUDY
Matilda makes a last-minute decision

Matilda K was buying a brand new two-bedroomed flat in Chelsea. The sale had not been easy one and it was nearly 12 weeks before she was in a position to exchange contracts. Just an hour before exchange of contracts was due to take place she received a phone call from the estate agent saying that the vendor wanted another £5,000. He said that the sale had taken so long that prices had now risen and that he had a queue of people who were prepared to pay a higher price for the flat. Matilda was furious. Her first instinct was to tell the developer to forget the whole thing. However, on reflection she recognised that property prices had risen in the area and that she would not be able to buy another flat for the same price. Furthermore, starting all over again would cause her considerable personal inconvenience. Matilda's previous job had been in Brussels and she was living in a hotel at her new employer's expense. With great reluctance Matilda agreed to pay the extra £5,000.

> Commenting on her experience, Matilda says, 'I felt that I was cheated out of £5,000 but it would have cost me a lot more to back out of the purchase and my vendor knew this so I just had to bite the bullet.'

EXCHANGING CONTRACTS

These days contracts are usually exchanged over the telephone and most solicitors will telephone immediately to let you know the good news. It's safe to open the champagne now. Things can go wrong between exchange and completion but it is extremely rare. I have dealt personally with only three cases.

In the first one the purchasers decided to end their marriage a few days before completion was due to take place. Neither party wanted the house and they ended up forfeiting their ten per cent deposit. In the second case, the purchaser's father-in-law refused to honour a promise he had made to lend money to fund the purchase after a family row. Again the ten per cent deposit was forfeited. In the third case, the vendor went bankrupt between exchange of contracts and completion.

Nevertheless there are a number of legal procedures that must be dealt with before completion can take place. The main ones are as follows.

Evidence of title

The vendor's solicitor will send your solicitor a copy of the deeds or a summary of their content. If your solicitor has any questions he will make 'requisitions on title', ie put them in writing.

Draft transfer/conveyance

The vendors' solicitor will send your solicitor a draft transfer (for registered property) or conveyance (for unregistered property). This is the deed which passes the vendors' interest in the property to you.

Mortgages

Your solicitor will write to your mortgage lender to ensure that the mortgage money is available in time for completion.

Engrossment of transfer or conveyance

When both solicitors are satisfied with the terms of the deed it will be 'engrossed', ie a final version will be prepared for signature by both sides.

Signing of final documents

You will be asked to sign the final documents and provide a banker's draft for any further money required to fund completion over and above your mortgage advance.

Final searches

Your solicitor will conduct a bankruptcy search in case the vendor has just been declared bankrupt (in which case the property would no longer be his to sell). He also conducts a Land Charges Search to ensure that no last minute charges have been registered against the property. These could affect the mortgage lender's security.

KNOWING WHAT TO DO BEFORE COMPLETION DAY
Choosing a removal firm

All removal firms are not the same. The cost of making the wrong choice could be the loss of furnishings and ornaments that have taken a lifetime to collect. The best way to choose a removal firm is by personal recommendation. Ask your estate agent, friends and colleagues if they can recommend a good one. Always get more than one quotation and be sure to base the final decision on reputation as well as on price.

Removals only versus full packing service
Most removal firms offer a variety of service levels, ranging from a full packing service where they will literally do everything, to a basic service where they provide only the lorry and a single working driver. You will need to think carefully about the service that you need and be sure that the quotations you get from different firms are all for the same level of service.

Insurance
Many otherwise reputable removal firms limit their maximum liability for loss or damage to an absurdly low amount, sometimes just a few pounds per item. There are two ways to get round this problem. The first is to arrange for the necessary additional cover through your own household insurer. The second is to find another removal firm.

Perhaps if more people did the latter the removals industry would be forced to start making proper arrangements for the protection of its customers.

Moving yourself

Moving yourself is hard work and it may not save you as much money as you think. Once you add up the cost of van hire and the hire of the chests or specialist removal cartons (without which things will get broken) you may well decide that the saving is not worth it. If you do decide to go it alone, these tips will help things to go smoothly.

◆ Van hire. Go to a large specialist depot. Many do an all-in removals package which includes van, carton and trolley hire. Remember that they will need to see your driving licence on the day of hiring.

◆ Van size. If in doubt get the larger one. A larger van will allow more careful packing and reduce breakages.

◆ Allow plenty of time. It will always take you longer than you think to move house – start early.

◆ Anticipate making more than one journey. The contents of an average three-bedroomed house often do not fit into a 7.5 tonne box van (which is the largest that you can hire without an HGV licence). Allow time for a second or third journey.

Arranging the utilities

Arrangements for the new house

Unless you want to move into your home by torchlight, arrangements must be made well in advance.

◆ Gas/electricity/water. Phone the new gas, electricity and water companies. Tell them that you are taking over the supply and that you do not want the service to be discontinued. Ask for written confirmation. Be sure to read the meters as soon as you arrive at the new property.

◆ Telephone. If your new property has the same exchange code, you will have the option of keeping your old phone number. If not you will usually be given a choice between taking over your vendor's old number or having a new one. Make sure of your arrangements well in advance and ask for written confirmation.

Arrangements for the old house

Be sure to contact all the utilities to inform them that you are moving. Ask for a final account to be sent to your new address. Don't forget to read the meters before you go.

Mail

The Post Office offers an excellent mail forwarding service at a very reasonable cost. It is well worth purchasing this service for at least a year to ensure that important post doesn't go astray.

COPING ON COMPLETION DAY

Such is the perversity of the home buying process that things can go wrong even on completion day itself. Although such problems are fairly rare, it is important to keep in touch with your solicitor throughout the day. Two specific problems are worth mentioning.

Delay in receiving the money

The money to fund the purchase of each property in the chain will almost certainly be sent by telegraphic transfer. In this age of satellite communications you might think that money could be transferred between banks instantly. You would be wrong. The system is terribly inefficient. It often takes several hours for funds to be transferred. What is more there is a shut-off time (usually 1 pm) after which any funds sent will probably not arrive until the next day.

Due to the inadequacies of the system, the non-arrival of the completion monies is a fairly common problem. If you do not receive the money for your sale you will not be able to complete on your purchase, indeed completion for the whole chain could be delayed until the next day. The inconvenience, cost and legal implications of this delay can be horrendous. Every purchaser in the chain will be contractually obliged to complete by a certain time of day (usually 1 pm). Should they not do so they will be legally liable for any extra expenses incurred by their vendor. The result can be a lawyer's field day with everyone blaming everyone else for the delay.

Avoiding a delay
Unfortunately there is not much that you can do to avoid this problem although it is worth phoning your solicitor at around 12 midday to check that everything is OK. If there is a problem you will have at least an hour to solve it.

Arguments over the release of keys

Until the vendors have received the completion money they will not release the keys to you. This can be extremely frustrating if your removal men are waiting about doing nothing. Unfortunately there is very little that you can do about it. You can try asking the vendors to release the keys, but in view of the awful consequences that could ensue if you moved into the property and were then unable to pay for it, they are very unlikely to agree to do so. If you are not able to complete on completion day, you may be able to claim compensation for any additional costs that you incur from your own purchaser or from your mortgage lender if they were responsible for causing the delay.

ARRIVING AT YOUR NEW PROPERTY

Congratulations. You have done it – but before you completely relax it is worth doing two last things.

Testing the services

Check immediately that you have gas, electricity, water and a telephone. If any of these services have been disconnected you will need to get onto the suppliers immediately.

Reading the meters

It is all too easy to get caught for the previous owner's bill. Check the meters and make a careful note of the readings as soon as you move in.

Checking the fixtures and fittings list

Make sure that all fixtures and fittings that should have been left have been. If something major has been taken in defiance of the contracted agreement you can threaten to sue for its return.

THE LAST WORD

Moving house will never be easy, but I hope that this book has *helped* you to avoid some of the common pitfalls. All that remains now is to enjoy your new home.

This book might serve one last useful purpose. Put it on a bookshelf so that if, at any time in the future, you find yourself thinking wouldn't it be nice to have an extra bedroom, you can look at the cover and ask yourself if it's really worth it.

Appendix

Cost of Selling and Buying in England and Wales

House Prices	Cost of Selling		Cost of Buying	
£80,000	Solicitor	£442	Solicitor	£467
	Estate Agent	£1,227	Land Registry	£60
			Searches	£186
			Stamp Duty	£0
	Total	**£1,669**		**£713**
£100,000	Solicitor	£460	Solicitor	£486
	Estate Agent	£1,472	Land Registry	£100
			Searches	£186
			Stamp Duty	£0
	Total	**£1,932**		**£772**
£150,000	Solicitor	£498	Solicitor	£527
	Estate Agent	£2,146	Land Registry	£150
			Searches	£186
			Stamp Duty	£1,500
	Total	**£2,644**		**£2,363**
£200,000	Solicitor	£541	Solicitor	£571
	Estate Agent	£2,819	Land Registry	£150
			Searches	£186
			Stamp Duty	£2,000
	Total	**£3,360**		**£2,907**
£300,000	Solicitor	£617	Solicitor	£654
	Estate Agent	£4,145	Land Registry	£220
			Searches	£186
			Stamp Duty	£9,000
	Total	**£4,762**		**£10,060**

Cost of Selling and Buying in England and Wales

House Prices	Cost of Selling		Cost of Buying	
£500,000	Solicitor	£740	Solicitor	£784
	Estate Agent	£6,741	Land Registry	£220
			Searches	£186
			Stamp Duty	£15,000
	Total	**£7,481**		**£16,190**
£750,000	Solicitor	£940	Solicitor	£1,000
	Estate Agent	£10,127	Land Registry	£420
			Searches	£186
			Stamp Duty	£30,000
	Total	**£11,067**		**£31,606**
£1,000,000	Solicitor	£1,326	Solicitor	£1,398
	Estate Agent	£13,374	Land Registry	£420
			Searches	£186
			Stamp Duty	£40,000
	Total	**£14,700**		**£42,004**
£1.5m	Solicitor	£1,680	Solicitor	£1,783
	Estate Agent	£20,098	Land Registry	£700
			Searches	£186
			Stamp Duty	£60,000
	Total	**£21,778**		**£62,669**
£2m	Solicitor	£2,170	Solicitor	£2,318
	Estate Agent	£26,990	Land Registry	£700
			Searches	£186
			Stamp Duty	£80,000
	Total	**£29,160**		**£83,204**

Compiled by University Of Greenwich

The Cost of Moving research is compiled using data from over 1,300 Estate Agents, Solicitors and removal companies who provided data to THE UNIVERSITY OF GREENWICH, School of Architecture and Construction.

Used with kind permission of The Woolwich

Glossary

Annexe. A self-contained portion of a large house.

Applicant. A potential purchaser enquiring for a property to buy.

Bay-fronted. A property where the windows protrude from the front wall.

Block insurance. A type of building insurance policy which covers all the flats in a building.

Box bay. A bay window built in an oblong shape with two 90 degree corners.

Canopy porch. A porch comprising a roof only with open sides.

Capped chimney. A chimney which has been sealed at the top to prevent the entry of birds and/or dampness.

Cavity walls. Two brick walls built with a small space between them. This form of construction provides much better stability and weather protection.

Chalet bungalow. A bungalow with some first floor rooms built under the slope of the roof.

Company move. A move with financial assistance from employers.

Contents insurance. An insurance policy that protects a householder in the event of their furniture or other contents being lost, damaged or stolen.

Contract. A legal document setting out the terms under which a sale will take place.

Corporate estate agents. Firms of estate agents who are

owned by the financial institutions.

Covenant. A restriction on the use of a freehold property (eg it must be used for residential purposes only).

Dependent sale. A sale to a purchaser who has to sell their property before being in a financial position to proceed.

Detached. A house which is not joined to any other building on any side.

Detailed planning permission. The permission for development according to detailed planning specifications.

Dis-instruction. A vendor advises they no longer wish their property to be offered for sale.

Dormer window. A type of window which protrudes from a pitched roof allowing the glass to be held in a vertical position.

Dot screen photo. A special type of photograph designed for clear reproduction on a photocopier.

Double bay. A property with two bay windows.

Double glazing. Two layers of glass held in place by a single frame usually to reduce heat loss through the windows.

Dry rot. A type of fungus which can cause serious damage to a building.

Endowment. A type of combined savings and life assurance policy often sold as a vehicle to repay a mortgage at a future date with interest only being paid during the term.

En-suite bathroom. A bathroom for the sole use of a bedroom and with a door that connects directly to it.

Exchange of contracts. The point at which the sale usually becomes binding.

Ex-council. A house that was originally built for rent by the local authority.

Financial consultant. Somebody who is qualified under the Financial Services Act to give financial advice.

Financial services. An umbrella term for mortgage arrangements and insurance policies which are offered to clients and customers.

Fixtures and fittings. A collective term that is applied to any removable fixtures or fittings which may or may not be included in the sale price.

Flat. A self-contained portion of a building with its own kitchen and bathroom facilities.

Flat roof. A horizontal roof often covered in felt which requires regular renewal.

Flying freehold. A freehold property, all or part of which is supported by another adjoining property as opposed to being connected to the ground.

Freehold. A property which is owned in perpetuity.

Gable. The triangular-shaped vertical portion of wall at the end of the roof.

Gas radiator central heating. A gas boiler which heats a property via panel radiators through which flows hot water.

Gas warm air. A type of heating system where a gas boiler is used to heat air which is circulated through ducts to each room of the property with the assistance of an electric fan.

Gazumping. When a vendor accepts a higher offer after agreeing a sale with a purchaser subject to contract.

Gazundering. When a purchaser reduces the offer that they have made for a property at the very last moment.

Ground rent. An annual rental made to the freeholder under the terms of a long lease.

Hard standing. A cement or tarmac area designed for the

parking of a motor vehicle.

Independent estate agents. Estate agency firms which are still owned by private individuals or companies that are not linked to a financial institution.

Integral garage. A garage which is built within the walls of the main property and could have access to the property via an integral door.

Joint sole agency. An agency where two or more agents agree to share the commission regardless of which of them achieves the sale.

Leaded light. The small panes of glass often seen in cottage windows.

Leasehold. A property that the owner will only be able to use for a certain term. Many leases are originally granted for 99 years. At the end of this time ownership of the property will revert to the freeholder.

Legal executive. Somebody who works for a legal firm undertaking legal work but is not a qualified solicitor.

Legal completion. The day upon which money is paid and the purchaser usually has the right to occupy the property.

Lettings. The renting rather than selling of property.

Licensed conveyancer. Somebody other than a solicitor who is licensed to undertake conveyancing work.

Link detached. A detached house with an attached garage which is attached to another adjoining building.

Listing. Property that has been taken onto the market for sale.

Loft conversion. A room or rooms which have been formed in what was originally the roof space.

Maisonette. A flat with its own front door which has access direct to the outside as opposed to via a communal hallway, or a two or more storey flat.

Memorandum of sale. A summary of the main terms and conditions for a sale which is sent out to the vendor, purchaser and both solicitors when a sale is first agreed.

Mortgage indemnity. An insurance policy which protects a lender from incurring financial loss in the event that a property is sold for less than the mortgage that is secured on it.

Mortgage offer. A binding promise by a mortgage lender to lend money to a purchaser of a property usually with conditions.

Mortgage retention. When the property requires work the mortgage lender will occasionally retain a portion of the mortgage funds until that work has been completed to their satisfaction.

Mortgage valuation. A valuation for the lender of mortgage finance.

Multi agency. The situation where two or more agents are instructed to sell a property on terms where the first agent to achieve a sale will earn the entire commission.

No chain. A sale where the vendor and purchaser are not buying or selling other properties.

Oil fired central heating. Central heating powered by an oil burning boiler.

Open fireplace. A fireplace designed for use with a coal or log fire.

Open plan. A house with no internal walls to separate the living room, the dining room and the kitchen.

Outline planning. The local authority has given approval for an outline scheme which is then followed by detailed proposals.

Penetrating damp. Dampness that is penetrating through

walls, usually as a result of a defect such as a crack or a leaking drainpipe.

Personal interest. An estate agent is not allowed to purchase a property that his/her employer is selling without declaring a personal interest to the vendors. Agents must also declare a personal interest when they are selling a property which they own through the firm that employs them.

Pitched roof. The traditional style of roof pitched at an angle and usually covered in slate or tiles.

Planning permission. Permission granted by the local council for development or a change of use to a property.

PMA. An abbreviation for the Property Misdescriptions Act.

Probate sale. The sale of a property where the owner is deceased.

Purlin. The timber that supports the rafters in a pitched roof.

Quarter back. A group of houses built in a square with two outside walls and two walls shared with the adjoining properties.

Reception room. An old-fashioned term to describe the main living rooms.

Render. A sand-and-cement coating applied to the external wall of a property and often painted or textured.

Repayment mortgage. A conventional type of mortgage where money is borrowed and repaid with interest over the full term.

Relocation. Moving to a different part of the country with financial assistance from an employer.

Re-pointing. The restoration of the mortar between the bricks on an external wall.

Repossession. A property that has been repossessed by the mortgagees due to the non-payment of the mortgage.

Retention. A sum of money which is held back by a mortgage lender until certain specified works have been completed to a required standard.

Rising damp. Dampness which is transmitted up from the ground due to a failure or absence of a damp course.

Roof trusses. The larger triangulated structures usually built of timber which support the main weight of the roof.

RSJ. A steel beam which supports the weight of a structure over an opening.

Sash windows. The type of window which slides vertically up and down.

Secondary glazing. Two layers of glass held in place by two separate frames.

Search. An enquiry that is made of the local authority to check that nothing adverse is likely to happen in the immediate vicinity (such as a new road scheme).

Septic tank. A method of disposing of sewage when a property is not connected to a main sewer.

Single skin extension. An extension with a wall constructed of a single layer of brick ($4\frac{1}{2}$" thick). Such extensions are usually not suitable for permanent habitation.

Sold subject to contract. An offer has been accepted but exchange of contracts has not taken place.

Skylight window. A window which is at the same angle as the pitched roof itself.

Sole agency. An agent who is appointed as the only agent who will be offering a property for sale during a given period.

Solicitor. Somebody who is qualified by the Law Society to give legal advice.

Split level. A house where each storey is built on more than one level, usually on a hillside.

Stone cladding. A thin layer of stone or imitation stone which is attached to the external wall of a property.

Storage heater. A type of electric heating usually using cheap electricity available at night and discharging throughout the day.

Structural engineer's report. A specialist report on a property where there is evidence of structural movement or a potential risk.

Structural survey. A comprehensive survey which reports in detail on the condition of a property.

Studio. A type of small flat comprising one room which is usedfor living, sleeping and cooking together with a separate bath-room.

Stud wall. An internal wall made from a wooden frame rather than brick.

Stone cladding. A thin layer of stone or imitation stone which is attached to the external wall of a property.

Survey. A visit to a property by a surveyor who compiles a report on the structural condition and/or value of a property.

Take-on. A property that has been taken onto the market for sale.

Tandem garage. A double-length garage where two vehicles are parked one behind the other.

Terraced house. A house that is joined to the adjoining buildings on both sides.

Thatched roof. A roof which is covered with straw or reeds rather than tiles.

Tile-hung. Tiles hung on a vertical wall either for decorative purposes or to keep out dampness.

Timber frame construction. Where the building is based

around a timber frame.

Timber treatment. Any treatment to the timber in a property, eg woodworm, dry rot or wet rot.

Title deeds. The legal documents that prove ownership of a property.

Touting. A direct approach to the vendors of properties which are being offered for sale by another estate agent.

Town house. A three- or four-storey house with integral garage occupying the ground floor. Usually found in town centre locations where living and parking space are at a premium and usually in a terrace.

Traditional construction. The traditional form of building where the external walls of the property are load-bearing and of masonry construction.

Under offer. An alternative term for a property that is sold subject to contract.

UPVC. An abbreviation for a particular type of plastic window frame.

Vacant possession. A property which will be vacant on completion day.

Valuation. When a potential vendor invites an agent to value their house with a view to putting the property on the market.

Vendor. The person who is selling a property.

Wall tie. A metal tie that connects the inner and outer sections of a cavity wall to improve the structural stability.

Wet rot. Wood that has rotted through being saturated by damp.

Index

If you want to know how ... to keep your home and your family
safe from crime

"There is a lot that the average person can do to protect
themselves, their family and their property. This book will teach
you how to perform a security review on your home and show
you what countermeasures you can take to ensure that you are
highly unlikely to be a victim of crime."

Des Conway

The Home Security Handbook
How to keep your home and family safe from crime
D. G. Conway

Surveys have revealed that when asked what people worry most
about for themselves and their family 45% of them said
'CRIME'. Crime statistics certainly indicate that people have
good reason to worry: A burglary takes place on average every 30
seconds in the UK.

Alarming though this and other statistics may be, this book will
show you how you can use them to reduce the risk of becoming a
crime statistic yourself. It will teach you how to audit and review
your home and lifestyle, to identify a range of vulnerabilities,
threats and risks and then show you how to provide effective
countermeasures to avoid the threat and reduce the risk.

The countermeasures suggested are designed to be realistic,
achievable at minimal cost and effort and simple enough to be
introduced or implemented by the average person.

Des Conway has over 20 years security experience, which
combines police service with commercial security consultancy.
He has experienced countless security reviews of domestic and
commercial properties, delivering reports highlighting
vulnerabilities, and recommending simple, affordable and
achievable countermeasures.

ISBN 1 84528 024 5

If you want to know how ... to keep yourself and your family safe from crime

Based on his experience as a security consultant and over 20 years police service, Des Conway describes a range of crimes against the person, offering advice together with over 600 countermeasures that the average person can take to avoid that crime.

The Personal Security Handbook
How to keep yourself and your family safe from crime
D G Conway

Des Conway will teach you how to perform a security review on various different aspects of your life to identify and resolve any threats, vulnerabilities and risks. It includes:

• Protecting yourself against credit card theft and fraud
• Protecting yourself and your children from physical harm
• Keeping your car secure
• Dealing with bogus callers and nuisance telephone calls
• Reducing the risks from terrorism

Quite simply, Des Conway's goal in this book is to help you identify the circumstances in which you are vulnerable and in everything you do, to take simple and reasonable steps to make sure that you don't become the victim of a crime.

ISBN 1 84528 056 3

If you want to know how ... to make your first property purchase a success

'The sense of achievement gained from buying a first property is tremendous. It is a momentous occasion, filled with pride and contentment.

'It is true that there is a growing trend and an ever expanding ability to buy property, but there is associated with it a mountainous capacity for critical mistakes. This book is intended for savvy investors who wish to evade such errors. By following the advice laid out in this book, conducting a thorough personal assessment, investigating properties worthy of purchase and exploring all the alternatives, you will find yourself able to buy a dwelling that meets your needs and one that provides financial security for the future.'

Tony Booth

The Beginner's Guide to Property Investment
The ultimate handbook for first-time buyers and would-be property investors
Tony Booth

This book provides an insight into many key issues; it explains what constitutes a sound investment, how you can examine your borrowing potential and create a golden credit rating, what mortgages are available and which are most suitable. It also discusses alternative property investment; buy-to-let, let-to-buy, renovation, buying property abroad, self-build and self-employed business enterprise; and shares generous amounts of inside information and well-kept trade secrets.

ISBN 1 85703 961 0

If you want to know how ... to build your own home

More and more people are setting out to build their own dream home. This book will help you turn your dream into reality by explaining the process, stage-by-stage.

'Here you will find the practical knowledge required to go beyond your aspirations, to take that first step and start building the perfect home. At the end of the day, you will acquire the home you want, rather than one forced upon you from a limited variety, designed and constructed by a builder whose only motivation is to profit from your purchase. Instead of having to fit into a house, you can finally make a house fit you!'

Tony Booth and Mike Dyson

Build Your Own Home
The ultimate guide to managing a self-build project and creating your dream house
Tony Booth and Mike Dyson

This book will guide you through the fundamental elements of the self-build programme, from identifying and assessing a suitable building-plot to arranging finance and contractors. It deals with architects and designers, surveyors, labourers and tradesmen. It explains how to obtain planning permission and where to find appropriate insurance protection whilst construction is underway. Essentially, this book provides you with the know-how you need to complete a successful self-build project.

ISBN 1 85703 901 7

If you want to know how … to be a property millionaire

TV star Annie Hulley has amassed a substantial property portfolio in just three years. In this book she explains how she achieved it, the mistakes she made along the way, and what she's gleaned from the experience.

'I now have a substantial investment property portfolio and that is the reason for writing this book, to show that from humble beginnings you too can achieve your goal of being a property millionaire.'

Annie Hulley

How to be a Property Millionaire
From Coronation Street to Canary Wharf
Annie Hulley

'A must-read book…a practical guide for anyone who has an interest in investing in bricks and mortar.' – OPP

'…loads of advice on getting on the property ladder in the UK, plus a section on holiday lets and second homes…and a chapter with advice on buying in foreign markets.' – Homes Worldwide

'Hulley's guide covers a huge range of subjects relating to buying property, including different types of mortgages, buying at auctions, buying off plan, tax liabilities, estate agents, holiday homes and much more. She's done her homework.' – Observer

ISBN 1 85703 857 6

If you want to know how ... to invest in the stock market

This book explains in plain English all there is to know about what affects share prices, how to avoid unnecessary risks and how to trade on the stock market, whether it's up or down.

Investing in Stocks & Shares
A step-by-step guide to making money on the stock market
Dr John White

'Will be a help to private investors...Gives an easy-to-understand guide to the way the stock market works, and how the investor should go about setting up a suitable investment strategy.' – What Investment

'If you have got money to spare, start by investing in the purchase of this book.' – Making Money

'User-friendly... Contains practical examples and illustrations of typical share-dealing documents...demystifies the world of stocks and shares.' - OwnBase

ISBN   1 85703 847 9

If you want to know how ... to manage a successful buy-to-let enterprise

'By empowering yourself with the information in this book, you will enjoy the financial and personal rewards that becoming a landlord can provide. You will also have the satisfaction of knowing that you are in full control of your most valued asset. The private rented sector is an exciting, stimulating and challenging arena for novice and professional alike; this book will guide you through its many facets and show you how to generate a considerable income.'

Tony Booth

The Buy to Let Handbook
How to invest for profit in residential property and manage the letting yourself
Tony Booth

'An excellent first purchase for anyone contemplating investing in the buy to let market whether they are proposing to manage the property themselves or to use an agent to do it for them. First class and good value for money.' – The Letting Centre (Letting Update Journal)

'An excellent piece of work that clearly and concisely encapsulates the fundamental issues... I will be seeking that the book is placed high on recommended reading lists.' – Philip R Gibbs, Life President of the Residential Landlords Association

ISBN 1 85703 864 9

How To Books are available through all good bookshops, or you can order direct from us through Grantham Book Services.

Tel: +44 (0)1476 541080
Fax: +44 (0)1476 541061
Email: orders@gbs.tbs-ltd.co.uk

Or via our website

www.howtobooks.co.uk

To order via any of these methods please quote the title(s) of the book(s) and your credit card number together with its expiry date.

For further information about our books and catalogue, please contact:

How To Books
3 Newtec Place
Magdalen Road
Oxford OX4 1RE

Visit our web site at

www.howtobooks.co.uk

Or you can contact us by email at info@howtobooks.co.uk